Football's
Faithful
Fans

Football would be nothing without the fans – men and women, girls and boys (perhaps even a few dragooned animals!) whose commitment has often been likened to religious devotion. So *Football's Faithful Fans*, which is raising vital money for African development projects through the Homeless World Cup, gives Scottish supporters (a number of whom are clergy, with others from rather different backgrounds) a platform to say what fitba' means to them: hopes, dreams, rugged belief and, sometimes, sheer desperation! It's funny, thoughtful and entertaining – a bit like the Beautiful Game itself. Whether you're a fan or not, and whether you follow football in Scotland or elsewhere, here is an enjoyable insight into what might be gently called 'supporter psychology'...

Iain Whyte, who has edited this collection, is a Church of Scotland minister, historian, academic ... and a long-suffering St Mirren and Scotland supporter. So he feels your pain. He really does.

Entertaining, informative, and giving those who buy it an opportunity to help change the lives of young people in Africa. This book reads well. Many thanks for putting it together and thinking of helping our African teams.

Petros Chatiza, Coordinator, Young Achievement
Sports for Development, Zimbabwe

This is fun to read and helps some brilliant African youngsters change their lives for the better.

David Duke MBE, Founder and CEO of
Street Soccer Scotland

Great to see the women's game and the Women's World Cup feature large in this collection ... and all for a great cause!

Alana Watson, football researcher
and marketer

As women's football is especially showing right now, the beautiful game belongs to us all ... so we all need to believe a bit more in Scottish football!

Paul Goodwin, Founder and CEO of the Scottish
Football Supporters' Association

Anyone whose life combines faith and football – and the personal trials that come with both – will enjoy this lovingly gathered collection of stories.

Graham Spiers, sportswriter and broadcaster

A serious yet light hearted book that puts football in perspective.

Richard Holloway, writer, broadcaster, former
cleric, and chair of Sistema Scotland

Football's Faithful Fans

Edited by Iain Whyte

Siglum

First published in August 2019

Siglum (an Ekklesia imprint)
235 Shaftesbury Avenue
London
WC2H 8EP
www.ekklesia.co.uk

Siglum

Siglum Managing Editor: Simon Barrow

Production and design: Bob Carling (www.carling.org.uk)

Cover image: Graham Maule

ISBN: 978-1-9161733-0-9

A Catalogue record for this book is available from the British Library.

The cover photograph shows Scotland's Kim Little scoring against Brazil on 8 April 2019. Scotland won 1–0.

Contents

Introduction

This is a book about what it means to believe in football. Not necessarily in a religious sense, though a number of the contributors to this volume also have involvement in that world.

We acknowledge that faith and Scotland's national game have been intertwined for long, and not always to the good of society. *Football's Faithful Fans* is about the many positive ways in which the Beautiful Game can touch people's lives, irrespective of their belief or ideology.

So the contributors to this wee book take a mainly light-hearted (and sometimes thoughtful) look at their own loyalties to belief on and off the pitch, and to how the sore trials of following their team have tested basic emotions and convictions in their lives.

All of us do so with a commitment to oppose any form of hatred to others, and to help put to death sectarianism, racism and other forms of hatred that can poison both sport and society more widely.

Thanks are due to the anti-sectarian charity Nil by Mouth and to the Scottish Episcopal Church's Global Partnerships Committee for their generous support, to Graham Maule for the cover design and Mel Young for providing the Foreword, to Simon Barrow and Bob Carling at Siglum for all the work and commitment given to bring this book to publication, to the Scottish Football Supporters Association for assisting with publicity, and to my wife, Isabel, for her continuing support. Last but by no means least to the authors for the rich contribution of articles (and poetry) that have made the whole enterprise possible.

All the proceeds from this volume will go to the Homeless World Cup's work in enabling young African teams to attend the annual tournament and provide opportunities for homeless young people to change their lives.

We hope that you enjoy reading this and helping to bring hope through friendship, pride, team work and sport.

Iain Whyte

Publisher's Preface

In welcoming *Football's Faithful Fans* to the world I find myself wearing two hats (or three, if you include my Dumbarton FC bobble hat!). I am the Managing Editor of Siglum, the Ekklesia Publishing imprint under which the book is appearing. But I am also, as it happens, Chair and co-founder of the Scottish Football Supporters Association (SFSA), which is among those bodies endorsing the charitable purpose underlying this collection – support for the Homeless World Cup's initiative in helping African teams to attend the annual tournament and providing opportunities for homeless young people to change their lives.

The SFSA has as one of its lead slogans the simple statement, "We Believe in Scottish Football". Of course, like the contributors to this book, we also believe in the game as a whole – and in supporting our friends and colleagues in Africa and across the world. Understood in this way, football is and should be an act of solidarity, shared belonging and common endeavour.

What gets called the Beautiful Game is also, of course, about competition. In the context of friendship and collaboration, that is perfectly healthy. When mired in narrow tribalism and prejudice, it can become something far less healthy – quite toxic, in fact. So what lies behind the stories and accounts in *Football's Faithful Fans* (quite a few written by religious believers, others by people of good faith but no religious conviction) is also a shared commitment to celebrating the positive impact of the game – and its connection to other, different aspects of our lives – as a sport with inherent values that stand firmly against sectarianism and every form of hatred.

As well as enjoying some good and amusing stories herein, also expect to be stimulated, intrigued (and maybe baffled!) by the different personal hopes and dreams people bring to football in Scotland and beyond. But above all, enjoy the fact that this book is also raising money to do good, build bridges and strengthen our common humanity.

Simon Barrow
Siglum/Ekklesia Publishing

Foreword

Keep the faith!

How many times have I heard that expression as we troop out of our football ground after a bad defeat or a loss in the derby or after we have been beaten again at Hampden on our way to what should have been Cup glory or worst of all after we have been relegated?

The scarf is thrown in the corner, head in hands. That's it, I've had enough, I'm never going back. My friend puts his arm around my shoulder: keep the faith, he says. My mood is gloomy as I look in the mirror: keep the faith, I whisper, but it's a challenge as any loyal football supporter will tell you.

The next day the sun shines. We win the derby, we get promoted, we win at Hampden and we play glorious attacking football. I don't know why I ever questioned myself. Life is wonderful until the day it starts raining and we start losing again. The glory of it all.

Football is a mirror of life. It teaches us to take nothing for granted. Life has ups and downs and we learn to cope with the good and bad days. We should always try and remain positive because as football teaches us: you can lose one day but you can always come back and win the next.

There are millions of people who are homeless throughout the world. Being homeless rips the soul out of people. It destroys self-respect and damages self-esteem. Confidence hits rock bottom. For many homeless people their only objective is to get through until tomorrow.

I do not understand how we have created a world where homelessness is so prevalent when there is so much wealth and ingenuity in the world. We have the collective power to change it if we want to. I believe that we can end homelessness if we have the collective will.

We all can do something. The Homeless World Cup which was born in 2003 is a very simple concept which uses football as a universal language to reach out to homeless people all over the world to engage them in an activity which can change their lives completely. The organisation has touched the lives of 1.2 million people since it started and works with over 100,000 homeless people across 74 countries each year. Football is a universal language which everyone understands, and which people can join with even if they are no good at it.

It gives a sense of belonging and a sense of purpose. 80% of the participants change their lives forever. At its core, the Homeless World

Cup helps to restore lost self-respect and helps build dignity.

When people are homeless they feel low all the time and lose any hope, but football helps build them up by saying that all of us have good and bad days in life and that they are no different. Don't give up – keep the faith. Just like football: you can lose one day and win the next. Football has real power to create change.

I'd like to thank Iain Whyte for putting this book together. He has been a fabulous supporter of the Homeless World Cup over the years and we are incredibly grateful. All the proceeds for this book will go to our partners in Africa to help them build their organisations to engage with more homeless people and potentially help them get to the Homeless World Cup each year.

Who thinks homelessness is a good idea? No one. So, why do we have it? Come on, let's end homelessness completely. Together let's win the game and make the world a better place. Keep the faith, as they say!

Mel Young MBE
President and Co-founder Homeless World Cup
www.homelessworldcup.org

Chapter 1

Beyond Winning

Joseph M Bradley

Many people recognise that football across various countries has resonances beyond the mere action of kicking a ball (or opponent) and trying to defeat another eleven people attempting to do the same to your team. In is in such a context that we can discern that football in Scotland provides a window to understand how people there see themselves and others, as well as saying something significant about the country's cultures, histories, religions, ethnicities, nationalisms and identities.

Winning at football is clearly what much of the sport is about, but if this was the only factor in attracting people to watch the game it would never have achieved the success it has over more than a century as a major part of modern 'leisure activities'. One might only need to ask some well thought out questions of those supporters of teams that rarely if ever experience success on the field of play, but who nonetheless, keep supporting 'their' club.

The answers to such questions would inform us that within clubs there are memories and family treasures, as well as community esteem, ethnic and national histories, politics and culture. As with many other sports and human activities, and varying greatly from club to club and country to country, there is also some, or a lot of, racism, ethnic and religious prejudice and bigotry, discrimination, inequality, bias, prejudice, stereotyping and xenophobia.

Beyond playing and a tiny minority of players and others making vast sums of money, these are amongst the big things that give football its attraction and lifeblood. Football both reflects as well as offers meanings and extensions to various facets of the everyday, beyond the football field and stadium.

It is in this vein that I have sat alongside many football fans that support clubs in Scotland, asked them to complete questionnaires and interviewed several hundred others; among them St Johnstone, Dunfermline, Dundee, Dundee United, Hearts, Hibernian, Glasgow Rangers, Partick Thistle, St Mirren, Aberdeen, Kilmarnock and Celtic –

as well too as Scotland's famous national followers in the Tartan Army.

Many of these supporters I have interviewed in their own environments as well as beyond in other countries. All of these clubs contain supporters that are passionate about their football.

Such research demonstrates clearly that supporters have deep-seated and multi-layered ideas about all manner of things that touches on this passion for the game – history, culture, nationalism, ethnicity, the administration of football and political and economic influences in and out with football and wider society. These are the obsessions, ideas, notions, beliefs, attitudes, actions, events and issues that take the game beyond a straightforward sports event on the field of play: the things that can give professional football meaning. The very things that have made the game of football the world's most successful ever team sport.

Joseph M Bradley is Senior Lecturer in Sport and Culture at the University of Stirling and a writer on Football, Ethnicity, Race, Religion, Community, Nationalism and Identity in Scotland

Chapter 2

All shall be Well

Martin Scott

All shall be Well, and all manner of things shall be Well.
                                    Julian of Norwich (not City) 1342–c.1416

I grew up in Motherwell in a family which had absolutely no interest in sport. I wasn't physically strong, being quite debilitated by asthma brought on by severe hay fever throughout the spring and summer, so my activities were largely housebound ones – hence my initial career as a musician. Life as a child very much centred around the local Baptist Church and playing the piano. Things like football were frowned on as rough and working class, though somehow I was allowed to watch cricket on the television during long summers shut inside. It is another sport with which I remain obsessed – but that's for another day.

Always a rebellious child – see the child, see the man! – I was determined to be different. My initial forays into football were essentially an act of resistance, something counter-cultural. I was 13 when I attended my first match, against Albion Rovers at Fir Park. My brother, who shared the general family outlook on football, was best friends with the son of the Chief Constable of Lanarkshire, Mr James K McClellan, who was responsible for policing at such events.

Since there was someone respectable in charge, I was allowed to go with them. What a revelation! Although I did not realise it at the time, Motherwell had been relegated to the old second tier of Scottish Football in April 1968 and were beginning their climb back to the top. The crowd seemed large to me as I sat in the higher reaches of the main stand, though it was probably around a thousand. Motherwell won 7–0 in a dazzling display of total football before its time – I was hooked!

Having discovered this new world, nothing was going to stop me from going back. My mother must have realised that resistance would be futile, even though she thought it a frivolous waste of time. If I had a friend with me I was allowed to go, as long as there was not a meeting of the Lanarkshire Society of Organists, which was a kind of family ritual about once a month. I remember sitting in Hamilton College of Education listening to some old man droning on about Rheinberger Sonatas for Organ, looking out the window across the Clyde valley, fretting at the sight of the floodlights at Fir Park where I knew we were pressing for glory.

My initial season at Fir Park was a triumph. We won the Scottish Second Division at a canter: Played 36; Won 30; Drawn 4; Lost 2; Goals for 112, against 23; Points 64. Champions, finishing 11 points clear of Ayr United. We were unbeaten at home, drawing twice. As I had no obvious way of attending away games, this meant that in my first season I never saw Motherwell lose. In 16 of our games we scored four or more goals, including two more scores of seven against Stenhousemuir and Berwick Rangers.

Like most religious conversions – and supporting Motherwell for me was exactly that – the first experience is the one which sets the default in terms of expectation. This is what football is really like: a trail of glory, songs of victory, ecstatic fans hailing the gathering of trophies. Motherwell was surely among the greats not only of Scottish, but of World football. Thus began what is now more than 50 years of following The 'Well through hell and high water (mostly hell!).

Although I did usually have a friend with me, watching football was pretty much ploughing a lone furrow against the odds. The sense of elation at saving up and buying my first Claret and Amber scarf was tempered by the totally blank faces and utter lack of interest back home. The next season, though it started brightly with a 1 – 0 win over Kilmarnock at Fir Park, was something of a let-down, with Motherwell finishing 11th in the First Division. A temporary setback, I decided. The true believer knows that better is only just round the corner – so surely soon we would be champions of Scotland and follow Celtic's recent success in being crowned kings of Europe.

A pattern was now established which would mirror much of life: 90% struggle, disappointment and despair, with 5% celebration. It is not the despair that kills you, though, it is the hope. Leading the newly formed Premier League in December 1975, only to fall away, finish 4th and fail even to qualify for Europe.

Reaching a cup semi-final in 1975 against local arch-rivals, Airdrieonians, much the inferior team, leading 1–0 before a late own-goal led to a replay, which we lost 1–0 after our goalkeeper broke the 'four-step' rule and gave away a free kick more-or-less on the goal line. Coming from 2–0 down to Celtic at half-time in the Scottish Cup third round to win 3–2 in 1976, only to lose out by the same score to a shockingly bad refereeing decision against Rangers at the semi-final stage.

There was plenty of despair too. As a young music teacher at Airdrie Academy I had to endure weekly taunts from the kids as we plunged towards the oblivion of relegation in 1979 under the management of Ally McLeod – he of Ally's Tartan Army fame – including a (then) record Premier League defeat by 8–0 at Aberdeen.

It was probably no bad thing, then, that 1979 saw me head off to Zurich to study theology and train for Baptist ministry. This was the start of 20 years spent out of Scotland and visits to Fir Park were few and far between until our return in late 1999. My study of theology there was transformative, giving me a depth of understanding of the gospel as good news to the poor. This helped me reinterpret my football-supporting experience.

Like God in Jesus, I was on the side of the underdog, not a glory hunter! It was my lot to suffer, with only the occasional glimpse of resurrection – this truly was a vocation. Everything in those 20 wilderness years away from Fir Park reflected this. Following Grasshoppers Zurich rather than the rich FC Zurich; moving to complete my PhD at Durham and going week about to Newcastle as they were relegated to the second tier and to Sunderland as they dropped to the third for the first time in their history!

Then to Manchester for ten years, where City became my permanent second footballing love and Maine Road my regular haunt in one of the worst phases of their history, the 1990s. I well remember losing a match against Bury as City slid towards the trapdoor to the Third Division. First a season-ticket holder ran onto the park and ripped up his ticket in the centre-circle. This was followed by a bad foul from City player Ged Brannan – so poor a player that City fans started chanting "Off! Off!" in the hope the referee might save us further despair.

Needless to say he was only booked. It won't surprise you either to discover that when I returned to take up my season ticket at Fir Park in Dec 1999, Mr Brannan was playing for Motherwell.

Those years away provided one shining beacon of joy – the Cup Final of 1991. Somehow I managed to get 6 tickets for the game, so the whole family, plus two friends from Newcastle days, stood together in the Mount Florida end at Hampden on Saturday 18 May as we watched Motherwell demolish Dundee United 4–3 after extra time to lift the cup for the first (and only) time in my life-time.

Goals from Ian Ferguson, Ian Angus, Phil O'Donnell, sadly no longer with us, and the talismanic Stevie Kirk brought the cup back to its spiritual home at Fir Park. Four more finals (2 Scottish and 2 League Cups) have followed since, but all have been lost. My wife, Jayne, sadly not one of the faithful but an occasional visitor – 3 times in 44 years – holds the unique record of never having been present when Motherwell lost. Perhaps I'll get her to come to the next final (see, the hope remains).

In the same way that the poor are always with us (John 12:8), so the burden of being the underdog seems unlikely to disappear in the foreseeable future. I must admit that the Manchester City experience has been a difficult one in that seeing a team you like winning things is exhilarating – yet somehow it doesn't feel the same because it is so tainted by the vast sums of money flung at it in a world of so much inequality and poverty. So there really is no danger that my first footballing love will ever be displaced, even if an odd (very odd) triumph appears somewhere on the way. Come on the 'Well!

Martin Scott has been a Baptist minister and a music teacher, a lecturer in New Testament and a Church of Scotland minister and administrator

Chapter 3

Ready for Anything

Tom Gordon

The day began like all the others that week in the Garfangana region of Northern Tuscany. Some of us were new to the area and some were seasoned Tuscan Travellers, but we were all prepared for another day of the appreciation of the beauty of the area, its fine food and wines and its generous hospitality and friendship. Late in the morning we found ourselves at the amazing *Eremo di Calomini* (The Calomini Hermitage).

It was hard to believe that this monastery, clinging like a limpet to the side of a rocky escarpment above the village of Gallicano, could be reached by anything other than a seriously unhinged mule, far less six intrepid travellers in a people-carrier! But reach it we did, to be greeted by the beauty of the church and the wonder of the view over the valley.

Once we'd explored the Hermitage and its surroundings, we settled down to lunch in a simple *Osteria* next door, not over-frequented by passing trade, we discovered – certainly not in a cloudy April – but welcoming and homely nonetheless. The food was good, the *Vino de la Cassa* excellent and the company convivial.

The bill had been paid and the wine about finished, when laughter began to rise as some of us swapped our party-pieces of kiddies' entertainment, the disappearing napkin ... the coin behind the ear ... the jumping mouse created from a gent's handkerchief. Not surprisingly, this hilarity attracted the attention of *il patrone* and the young lady who'd served us – the owners, Luca and Sara, we learned. In passable English they expressed a willingness to learn from our funny games something new to offer children – especially children of Rwanda with whom they'd worked before, and to whom they would shortly return.

Soon they were recounting stories of the €15,000 they'd helped raise locally, the nursery school accommodation their money had provided for 160 children, the building project which had been completed in three weeks; the charity which underpinned the work Before long we were gathered round a laptop to be moved and amazed as we saw picture after picture of the Rwandan children.

What could we do? Spontaneously we gathered a sizeable donation for Luca and Sara's next project in Rwanda. They were embarrassed and grateful, and, insisting we wait for a bit, Sara delved into the bottom of a cupboard and unearthed with triumph a bag of simple, wooden Rosaries. Giving one to each of us, she explained that they had been made by the Rwandan children for her to take back home to help with their fundraising. It was our turn to be embarrassed.

Now, Rosary Beads are not a common artefact for a Presbyterian! But I explained to Sara that I would take the Rosary home to the people I worked with in my hospice.

"I'm a chaplain, a *Pastore*," I tried to explain, "in a hospice."

She shrugged. "Pastore, yes, this I know," she offered. "But hospice, I do not understand."

"I work with people who are dying of cancer," I replied.

Sara smiled gently. "Cancer," she whispered, "yes, now I know. I have had cancer too."

We looked at each other for what seemed an age. I didn't know what to say or do. But I opened my arms and held Sara in a deep embrace. Her parting gift to me was the *whole* bag of Rosary Beads. "For your hospice people," she said. "I know where I can get some more."

Later in the day we stopped off at our village deli. We'd had a lovely meal in a local restaurant the previous evening (owned by the same people) and promised ourselves we'd stock up on some local salamis and cheeses on the way home. Part of the attraction was meeting up with Paulo again. Paulo was a real character, who, as 'Mister Entertainer', with broken English and a more than complete personality, had shared much hilarity with us at our evening's meal.

So, amid more joking and laughter, we bought our local produce, and, clutching our goodies, were soon ready to go. In the international language of football, I'd discovered that Paulo was a Juventus supporter, and as Fiorentina – their arch rivals – were to be playing Rangers in the semi-final of the UEFA Cup the following week, I reckoned the travelling Rangers fans might do well with an extra, local voice. So, with a flourish, I presented Paulo with my best Rangers shirt, and *insisted* he become a temporary Rangers' supporter against the might of Fiorentina!

There was raucous laughter, back-slapping, posing for photographs and exchanging of promises of undying friendship.

So *that's* why a Presbyterian hospice chaplain went out with a

Rangers shirt and came back with a bag-full of Rosary Beads! And that's why a simple, wooden, Rwandan Rosary is now my constant companion.

I had no chance! From as early as I can recall – and that's about the age of six – I've supported Rangers. But why should a little Teuchter laddie from Fort William (a town which, at that time, didn't even have a team in the Highland League, and where Shinty was the predominant sport anyway) become a died-in-the-wool Blue Nose? Simple! Enshrined in the family folklore (centred round regular holidays at my granny and grampa's in Paisley) was this irrefutable fact – my granny's cousin was none other than the great Torry Gillick, and he'd played for Rangers!

"Torry Gillick?" I hear you ask? Who? But it was a name for me which emerged from the land of myth and legend – at least my granny made it so for a wee starry-eyed boy. 'I remember crawling through the legs o' the fowk wi' ma twa sisters tae watch Torry play fur Stonehouse Violet when he wis a laddie, son," she would tell me. *Stonehouse Violet,* eh? Another name enshrined in romantic lyricism.

Torrance 'Torry' Gillick, hailed from Airdrie. My granny's family were all from Lanarkshire mining stock, with names of towns and villages like Larkhall, Stonehouse, Coatbridge, Airdrie creating in my mind lands of wonder and delight. Torry Gillick was born in 1915 and was signed for Rangers at the age of eighteen by the then manager, Bill Struth, after excelling with Glasgow's Junior football team, Petershill.

He won a Scottish Cup winners' medal with Rangers in 1935, but was sold in the summer of that year to Everton for a then club record fee of £8,000, playing for the Merseyside club till the outbreak of war in 1939, winning a League Championship medal and being capped five times for Scotland as an Everton player.

During the Second World War Gillick 'guested' for hometown Airdrieonians and Rangers, and when hostilities ended in 1945, Bill Struth brought him back to Ibrox, making Gillick the only player Struth signed twice. He became a regular feature in the famous post-war Rangers side, forming a great partnership on the right wing with Willie Waddell.

"See wee Torry," my granny would intone, "he *made* Waddell, so he did. Wi'oot ma cousin, Willie Waddell wid hae dun naethin', naethin' at a'."

I went to my first Rangers game when I was nine, an Old Firm

'Ne'erday' game at Ibrox on 1 January 1959. I remember little of that, apart from wearing the Rangers socks I'd got from my granny for Christmas, being lifted over the turnstile into what was then 'The Family Enclosure' in front of the main stand at Ibrox, rivers of pee running under my feet from the top of the terracing, my father swearing – not something I'd heard a Kirk Elder do before – and Rangers winning 2–1. Rangers went on to win the League Championship that season by 2 points from Hearts, with Celtic languishing in sixth place behind Motherwell, Dundee and Airdrieonians – oh, happy days! I genuinely felt that my attendance at my first Old Firm game was the catalyst for Rangers' greatness!

At a very early age I perfected a party-piece, which I was more than happy to offer to any assembled company at the drop of a Rangers bunnet. I could recite my favourite Rangers team from the early 1960s – Niven; Shearer; Caldow; Greig; McKinnon; Baxter; Henderson; McMillan; Miller; Brand; and Wilson. And as I offer unsuspecting friends the benefit of my party-piece even now, I can see every player's face, every mazy dribble, every headed clearance, every crunching tackle, every wonderful skill in my mind's eye.

I held down the right back berth for three years in the New College team when I was training for the ministry. (The left back was an evangelical Ulsterman who wore glasses when he played, with lenses in them that were as thick as the bottom of a Champagne bottle.

"See these specs," he would remind us regularly in the changing-room before and after a game, "they're made of glass so tough you could shoot a point-two-two bullet at them and it wouldn't go through." I declined to ask him what kind of football matches he played in back home in Belfast.) I turned out occasionally in charity games for a 'ministers and priests eleven' against a team of ex-professionals for the two years I was in Easterhouse.

We once played in a set of borrowed strips from Ibrox. I wore Sandy Jardine's Number 2 shirt. I can feel the tingles even now as I think about it. And in one game I played against the aforementioned Bobby Shearer and Eric Caldow, Rangers and Scotland's legendary full-back partnership of the 1960s. I was star-struck. Bobby Shearer stood on my foot as I tried (in vain) to get the ball off him – painful but wonderful at the same time.

Ah well. We've had our good days and our bad ones, that's for sure. But good days will come again. That's what being a loyal Blue Nose is all about, isn't it. "Ready" for anything, still hoping, still believing.

Tom Gordon *is a Church of Scotland minister, former hospice chaplain, and writer*

Chapter 4

A Grand Old Team to See

Martin Mann

In the centenary season of the foundation of Celtic Football club I made my entrance into this world and was destined to a lifetime allegiance to a team that my family had supported from time immemorial. Celtic had completed "the double" under the management of Billy McNeill and my father had attended the Scottish Cup final on 14 May 1988, but far more importantly for him (and for me) I made my appearance on 21 September.

There were perhaps two things that I was bound to inherit: support of Celtic FC and membership of the Roman Catholic faith. I haven't stopped practising either over almost thirty years. The faith part wasn't always voluntary as a child and my mother would at times have to remind me of that! But the lyrics "it's a grand old team to see" have always proven true for me.

My father assures me that my first Celtic game was before the take-over of Fergus McCann but it was after his arrival that I became a season ticket holder in the temporary West stand while the stadium was being rebuilt. I remember the enthusiasm as I travelled to the game with my dad and uncle in the car. We parked in the East End around the corner from St Michael's Church, a short rotund woman shouted in a Glaswegian accent that she'd "watch the car for you Mr". Incidentally she is still there 23 years later and I taught her son.

I was then guided through the strange streets with huge buildings; we didn't have tenements in Coatbridge you see, towards the stadium with crowds of men and boys, with the odd woman, all heading in the same direction. Then suddenly Celtic Park appeared in front of me. My first league game of the season was a 1–1 draw with Motherwell. Tommy Burns was Celtic manager and the football was fast and enjoyable, although not always successful, as what should've been my second home game proved – a 2–0 defeat at the hands of Rangers. I wasn't permitted to attend these games because my mother and father both agreed that it wasn't the right environment for a seven-year-old. As a father myself, I now agree, but at the time I was livid.

My first home victory came on 7 October 1995 in a 2–1 win against Patrick Thistle but there was a price to be paid. My father burst my lip celebrating as he threw his arms out and caught me in the face. As a way to buy my silence and settle me down on the journey home he bought me a burger from 'Rab Haw's kitchen'.

Alas, not only did I experience my first Celtic win at home but also my first bout of food poisoning. We've never been back there for a burger in the 23 years since and I've never been a fan of burgers from any fast food vans.

My attendance at Celtic park continued most seasons as the stadium was completed although I took a short hiatus in the last two years at secondary school and throughout my time at university. My attendance at weekly mass did not falter, even while at university, as I studied a concurrent teaching degree to become a Religious Education teacher.

There are many highlights of supporting Celtic in what has been an extremely successful period for the club but surprisingly my great joy is to be found in the days of a particularly sparse period for the trophy cabinet ... the Barnes/Dalglish saga. My only living grandparent, my 'Gana', has two friends who are avid Rangers fans but who were like an additional set of grandparents to me growing up. Irene and Malk paid for my 'Huddle Club' membership as boy which resulted in me being selected as an 11 year old mascot for the Bayern Munich –v- Celtic Millennium game.

This was a mind-blowing experience for a child and proved to be as exhilarating for my father as it was for me. The first autograph in my brand new autograph book was none other than the legendary Danny McGrain. To tell the truth I didn't have any idea who he was as I asked for his autograph. The legend asked me if I did and laughed when I replied, "I know you're really important because my dad can hardly speak 'coz he saw you!"

That evening my autograph book was inundated with stars from the Celtic team, the Munich team and also the remaining Lisbon Lions who were all in attendance for the celebratory game. That autograph book still holds pride of place in my study and because of dad's job the great names that it holds are quite extraordinary, including the likes of: Kaka, Seedorf, Ronaldo and Nesta but my favourite has to be the great Paulo Maldini. I remember standing in the tunnel full of excitement as Tom Boyd held my hand, and as we walked out onto the holy ground of paradise before kick-off, I prayed that I didn't lose my footing and make an eejit of the whole family who were either in the ground watching or trying to do so on TV. The prayers must've been answered because nobody made any visible mistakes.

That year was also my penultimate as an altar boy in St Bartholomew's parish Coatbridge as I gave up in S2 only making guest appearances for weddings and funerals. Fr Hugh Kelly was parish priest with the renowned Fr George Donaldson, a school pal of my Granda, in residence. Fr Donaldson would regularly visit our home which was a stone's throw from the chapel house especially if he knew we had the football on TV rather than the radio. Fr Kelly would often leave the radio on in the vestry during mass and would send one of the altar servers in during the Mass to keep him updated with the score. The only time that you could rely on his homily being short was when Celtic were playing and he wanted to catch the score!

I taught in the East End of Glasgow since August 2012. I never thought when I started teaching that my classroom on the second floor would have a wonderful view of Celtic Park nor that one of the house groups in Glasgow's oldest Catholic secondary school would be named after Celtic's founder, Brother Walfrid. The reason for this is found in the Marist Brother's connection with founding the Academy and managing it until the late 80's and with establishing Celtic FC to fund charitable endeavours in the East End. Andrew Kerins, the man from County Sligo who founded Celtic, was headmaster of our associated primary Sacred Heart hence the reason for the pupils selecting Br Walfrid along with St Enoch, St Ninian and St Andrew as our school house names. The location of the job is handy for home games of an evening, especially champions league games which sadly will not feature at Celtic Park this season of 2018–19. We can always look forward to the group stages next year after we beat Gerard's Rangers to secure eight league titles in a row.

I still attend matches with my father who has now retired due to injuries suffered in the Clutha Vaults tragedy while on a work's night out. We're fortunate to share our love of football and faith probably more so now than ever because it was such a close call him making it through. I've no doubt at all that his Guardian Angel was working overtime that night and that the intercession of Saint Padre Pio in particular gave us what we prayed for when we heard the news. It's strange now that as we attend games, often after participating in the 12pm mass in St Patrick's Coatbridge, that the roles are slightly reversed from that first game of mine in 1995.

I do the driving now and tend to have to slow down my pace a little for the old fella to keep up as we walk amongst the crowds heading to the game. I was so excited and nervous about making that first journey into Glasgow to watch our family's team. I always felt safe though because my dad, whom I idolise now as much as then if not more so, was there to show me the way and usher me to my seat. He was so big and strong and knew everything about everything albeit his choice of fast foo d left a lot to be desired!

I can't help but wonder if he thought the same about my Granda when he took dad to his first game or if my wee girl Orlagh will think the same of me when I take her to her first game in a few years' time- she's 6 months old as I write this so still a bit young yet. There's two things she's bound to inherit from me: support of Celtic FC and membership of the Roman Catholic faith. So the wheels keep turning and it's still "a grand old team to see."

Martin Mann taught RE at St Mungo's High School, Glasgow. He now works for Missio, a charity of the Catholic Church

Chapter 5

Sunshine On Leith

Lesley Orr

Picture the scene: it's Wednesday 26 August 1970 and on a balmy Edinburgh evening, a dad and his twelve year old have joined the throng of Hibs fans heading along Albion Road. A pub door swings open and disgorges its unmistakable heady, hoppy aroma, swirling around a bunch of men who laugh and swear beerily as they push past, rushing towards the stadium which suddenly looms into view behind the tenements.

There's a low thrumming, getting louder, and the child can feel it reverberating through the ground as they join the queue, go through the turnstile and approach the stairs leading up to the East Terrace. They're carried along with the horde, the noise intensifies ... and then they're in, high up under the television gantry – part of a heaving, singing, swaying crowd of 25,000 bodies.

The floodlights are on, the teams run out and within seven minutes the sublime Pat Stanton has scored. The Hibs fans go wild, and I'm one of them, cheering with delight. By half time, the score is four nil, and Aberdeen are reeling as Hibernian FC turn on the style to set up a League Cup quarter final tie against Rangers. I'm reeling too – overwhelmed by the scale and the passion and the unlikely glamour of a packed Easter Road, and thrilled by the flowing football my team are playing.

It's my first visit to a live senior game and I'm well and truly hooked. The actor Dougray Scott was once interviewed about being a Hibs supporter, and recalled his own initiation: "It was like going to a church for the first time, but with noise. It was a thing of beauty. Even now, when I walk up the steps on a Saturday afternoon and see the pitch, the hairs on the back of my neck stand up." I know exactly what he means.

But it wasn't supposed to be like this for me. It's a time honoured custom for support of a football team to be passed down through the generations, and for parents (usually fathers) to indoctrinate their offspring (traditionally their sons) into the mysteries and rituals of fandom from an early age.

My dad Jack grew up in Dumbarton – a true Son of the Rock. He was a talented footballer, playing in goal for Scottish Universities and capped for Scotland amateurs before becoming a Civil Service Stroller when he moved to Edinburgh as assistant minister at the Old Kirk in West Pilton. My uncle Clem was also a gifted footballer, and while still a teenager found himself at the centre of a bidding war between the city rivals. He was at Easter Road and literally about to sign his name on the contract when the Hearts scout swooped (they always swoop) and took him across town to Tynecastle: Clem the Jambo was a happy boy! Whatever the reason, Jack gave his allegiance to Hearts, and duly passed the affliction on to my brothers, who in turn have ensured that there are maroon clad Orrs all over the place.

But that's a story about boys, and I was a girl growing up in a time and place which very definitely saw football as a man's game. Like every other community in Scotland, Oxgangs in the 1960s was full of wee boys being socialised into acceptable Scottish masculinity by learning to chase and kick heavy leather balls – in streets, parks and school pitches – and on Saturday afternoons partaking of the rites of passage appropriate to whichever tribe they had been initiated into.

This world was not only indifferent to girls, but was about creating a culture which by definition seemed designed in every way to exclude us. It wasn't as if my parents discouraged me from enjoying football – we were a sporty family, and Mum was as competitive and passionate as anyone I have ever known, though football wasn't really her thing – maybe years of being made to go along and watch her wee brother Clem playing for Broughton Star had something to do with that. But I liked our back garden games of three-and-in, and reckoned I could have been quite good – if only I could have joined in the school playground games, and if only someone had given me a bit of coaching and encouragement, instead of making fun of my efforts.

So I grew up being the annoying wee sister (no wonder my brother David and his pals regularly tied me to the clothes pole) and all the while watching *Sportscene*, laughing at Fat Sam Leitch, reading match reports in the *Sunday Post*, learning the lingo and finding every reason I could to pick a quarrel with David. By the late 1960s, I had discovered that having a go at his beloved Hearts was a sure-fire way to needle him.

The 1969–70 season was my epiphany. Down Leith way a team full of talented players were playing classy football, especially a particularly groovy young winger whose reputation as the 'new George Best' went well beyond his silky ball skills. (And by the way, I did see the original George Best playing in a Hibs shirt). It would be an exaggeration to say that Peter Marinello converted me, but he certainly helped! Even Dad had to admit they were a decent team, and so it was that I persuaded him to take me to my first live match that August evening. There was no turning back.

Becoming a Hibs fan was a formative part of my adolescent assertion of autonomy and identity. I wanted to mark myself as a girl who loved the beautiful game, who understood the rules, who appreciated the kind of 'total football' which, at their best, made Turnbull's Tornadoes of the 1970s such a joy to behold (and why my favourite footballer of all time was Dutch number 14, Johan Cruyff).

I also wanted to belong to the tribe, but that required an active, counter-cultural decision to enter what was then an obsessively, often aggressively masculine world. I was delighted to find a female school friend who shared my passion for Hibs, and for several seasons in the early seventies, Jackie and I paid our 50 pence to stand on the terraces with thousands of singing, shouting, smoking, swearing, sweating, spitting men. Then there was the pissing into beer cans. Anyone who disputes that girls and women were alien invaders into that 1970s world has obviously never availed themselves of the female toilets under the old East Terrace! Mostly we were treated with gruff but benevolent good humour as a curiosity, but we had to put up with plenty of mundane sexism, and sometimes were really in harm's way – especially going home after matches.

Football fandom is a much more family friendly experience these days, although as a gender historian and feminist activist, I'm well aware of the continuing correlations between football and toxic masculinities. But I love it that Hibernian were in the vanguard of supporting and developing women's football in Scotland; I love it that Leeann Dempster is such an impressive and respected Chief Executive. And I loved seeing hundreds of wee girls – some of them tiny – with their parents and brothers at the 2016 League Cup Final.

That was the one we lost to Ross County. Hibs have a bad habit of being runners up, but by far my most traumatic experience was at Hampden for the 1972 Scottish Cup Final. I won't mention the score, but we left after Celtic scored their fourth. There were two more finals between the teams that year, and Hibs won both … just not the one that really mattered. Nevertheless, I've celebrated some famous Cup victories over the years – and not all of them involved Hibs.

We were living in Kirkcaldy when Raith Rovers had a divinely kissed run to the 1994 League Cup Final and miraculously beat Celtic on penalties. It was a moment of supreme joy for the whole community. Our five-year-old son was there. It instilled totally unrealistic expectations in his young heart: he's still waiting to dance in the streets of Raith once more. And here's a confession: I was with the Orrs cheering the Jambos on their 1998 victory parade to Gorgie, genuinely delighted for my dear Dad, sporting his maroon and white wig; the Hearts supporter who was happy to watch Hibs with me; the man who never swore or raised his voice at a bad decision; the hospital chaplain who befriended my favourite Hibs players (remember Cropley?) when they were crocked.

Which brings me to that pinnacle of long delayed and totally ecstatic gratification for all Hibs fans everywhere: the glorious May day in 2016 when we finally won the Scottish Cup, defeating Rangers 3–2 in a wonderful match. The emotions I experienced in the minutes between Gray's header and the final whistle were as intense as anything in my life, and joining the next day's celebrations when half a million people turned Leith Walk green and white was profoundly moving. You don't need me to tell you that Hibernian are the coolest club in Scotland, and we surely have the best anthem. If Scottish football sometimes exemplifies the worst elements of quasi-religion, it can also embody the best of the collective human spirit. So thank you, thank you, thank you, thank you Hibs for putting Sunshine on Leith.

Lesley Orr *is a writer and historian*

Chapter 6

The Joy of the Jags

Erik Cramb

My job took me to Kingston Jamaica in 1981, my eldest son Donald was just three years old, and I still had not taken him to Firhill to see my beloved Jags and, of course, the greatest goalkeeper on the planet, the 50 times capped Alan Rough.

When we left for Jamaica, as a typical Glaswegian, if anyone had told me cricket was exciting then I would have recommended them to a good psychiatrist. That was before Donald and I saw the then fearsome West Indies fast bowlers operating in the exciting and colourful caldron of Sabina Park.

Despite all the stories I had fed him about the magic of Alan Rough, by 1984 when it was time to return home, Donald wanted to be a wicket keeper rather than a goalkeeper. It was clearly time to re-introduce him to the true faith in Firhill for thrills. Sadly though, by this time Alan Rough had departed, first to Hibs and then to Celtic ... and Thistle had been relegated.

After the sunshine of the Caribbean, a November drizzle in Maryhill was just a tad short of being attractive, and Brechin City were not the most alluring of opponents, but these were the ingredients of Donald's Firhill baptism. After 85 minutes in the limb numbing cold and gloom, Thistle score. Donald jumps and shouts and hugs me. The drizzle evaporates – well it seemed like it. 'Upbringing' is a strange old mix. This is part of our culture, taking your boy to the match. Although he's been living in England for 10 years now, Donald still keeps the faith and the Jags' result is the first one he looks for every Saturday. It is truly Joy – nae maybes about it.

Naming the Deserters
For five years, from 1984 to 1989 my son Donald and I hardly ever missed a Partick Thistle home game at Firhill. Just before I moved to a new job in Dundee, I had mentioned to a club official that we would not be coming as regularly in future. To my astonishment, in the next match programme there were a couple of lines wishing Donald and I

well in our move north to Dundee. As we took our seats in the stand I got a tap on the shoulder from one of the regulars who sat behind us. When I turned round he said, "Oh my God, things must be bad, I see we're naming the deserters now!" On the whole we Jags supporters are a tolerated species, that is except when we are winning games that we're not expected to win.

My first parish was St Thomas' Gallowgate which had within its boundaries, Celtic Park, or Parkhead or Paradise if you were of the Celtic persuasion. As the parish minister, and known to be a Partick Thistle supporter, I was invited to a game when Thistle were the visitors. Which was great – hospitality, best seats and all that. Then, did Thistle not score first and I was on my feet shouting 'Ya beauty'. I look around, I was alone on my feet, and every seat around me was filled by less than benevolent glares. I quietly sat down to nurse my joy more privately. Not surprisingly though Celtic ran out 4–1 winners and I was being well tolerated again.

Years later in Dundee, I was invited by the Lord Provost to Tannadice, the home of the then highly successful Dundee United. He was an avid 'Arab'. Again the Jags delightfully 'embarrassed' me, not only by scoring first, but by winning the match. As I was being driven home in the civic limousine with a grumpy Lord Provost, I was reflecting – not on the Jags' victory as you might imagine – but on my half-time pie. Actually not the pie itself which was pretty good, but the fact that it was served up on a china plate. "Your half-time pie on a china plate," I said to myself; "how far is that from your working-class roots?" Thinking about that now, I wonder just how far our wonderful game has traveling from its roots amongst the people?

Jackie Husband and the Turin Shroud

Jackie Husband was Partick Thistle's legendary half back in the post war years. Sadly he was only capped once for Scotland – against Wales in 1947.

Scottish Television programmes used to feature a late night programme appropriately called *Late Call*. It was a five-minute programme before the TV shut down for the night and featured a minister or a priest sitting in a huge leather chair giving a wee homily to the cameras. I did this on a number of occasions. I have to confess that rarely did I get much feedback except from people I knew.

For one of these programmes I borrowed Jackie Husband's sole Scottish jersey to use as a visual aid. The truth is, I cannot for the life of me remember the point I was trying to make, but I'll never forget one phone call I got from a complete stranger. "Rev Cramb," he said, "I watched you last night with that football jersey and to look at the way you handled it, it could have been the Turin Shroud!" Well for me that jersey was pretty sacred!

Erik Cramb *is a former parish minister and workplace chaplain in Dundee*

Chapter 7

Hit it, John!

David McLachlan

My name is David McLachlan and I am a St Mirren fan. Those words sound like an opening confession at an addiction meeting – and in some ways they are. To support a team that isn't always doing very well is a kind of addiction, especially if it involves going to all the games you possibly can and in all weathers. It even costs actual money!

I wasn't always a St Mirren fan, though. As a young boy I did some growing up in Dunfermline. Our family lived on Garvock Hill (which overlooked East End Park) and though I was deemed too young to go to the games, I wasn't too young to climb on to the top of our garage and look down over the rooftops to watch half of the matches. Before Dunfermline built their main stand one half of the pitch was visible from the houses above.

There wasn't much fun in that, but back in the day, Dunfermline were a fairly good team. George Farm had taken over from Jock Stein who had really raised the profile of the club, and I watched them win the Scottish Cup in 1967 beating Hearts – and they even got to the semi- final of the European Cup Winners Cup in the next season.

Our family made the move to Paisley, and my dad suggested I should support a 'local' team. As a Glaswegian he suggested *his* team – Rangers. We made a couple of trips to Ibrox, but there was something about Rangers – maybe the atmosphere, or the fact that they were so rich or dominant in the game, that I didn't gel with them.

Then one November day in 1968 we went to a match in Paisley itself, where Rangers (the biggest Scottish team at that time) faced St Mirren (a team that had just gone 33 games unbeaten). Something had to give. My father and I entered the stadium ostensibly as Rangers fans. By the end of that dramatic match (which St Mirren won 1–0) I decided that St Mirren was the team for me. Also, I noted the colours on their strip meant I didn't have to buy a new scarf.

Over the years the list of our players ran like a who's who of world football. Players like Bone, Stickroth, Money, Yardley, Beckett, Abercrombie, Torfasson, Hewitt, Potter, Cheesy – household names every one, all of whom (I'm sure you'll agree) could walk into any World Top XI. The Brazilian Ronaldinho (anxious to taste football in Europe) almost signed for St Mirren in 2001, and that move only broke down because of his involvement in a passport scandal back home. The very next year, Ronaldinho won the World Cup with Brazil. Not bad, but would he have broken into the St Mirren first team? Probably not.

In truth St Mirren *have* won some things over the years. We were the first UK team to win a European trophy. We won the first Barcelona Cup, years before Celtic's win over Inter Milan. Our victory over Dundee United in 1987's Scottish Cup Final was achieved by 11 Scots-born players – the last time this is ever likely to happen.

At an early stage in the club's history, (which predates my support) St Mirren decided to be generous and give an advantage to their opponents by refusing to learn how to take throw-ins. This has become a proud tradition at the club and to this day St Mirren players have no idea how to respond when the ball goes out at either side of the pitch.

For some reason the SFA has never liked the team from Paisley and every week they send out the most incompetent and biased referees to our games. As a direct result of this policy, faith is needed to hope that we can rise above the odds that are stacked against us. On a very cold and miserable day some years back I stood shivering with my two young sons at Love Street, as another game slipped away from the Buddies - thanks in large part to poor refereeing decisions. The children were close to tears, and I felt very sorry for them. On noticing my forlorn kids, someone asked me, "Why do you take your boys to this rubbish?" And suddenly the answer came to me. "To teach them about injustice" I replied defiantly.

Most people assume that the big division in Scottish football is between Rangers and Celtic. Certainly in terms of supporters, they easily account for the biggest numbers. But to my mind the real gap is between these two and all the other clubs. The Old Firm may not have the resources to achieve much in European competitions but domestically their stranglehold on the game mean that no other team in the country can keep up with them or seriously challenge their dominance. It works in a cycle. The team that wins gets the most money, which means that they are able to buy the best players which means that they are able to win again and so it goes. A good young player in one of the 'smaller' teams will be easily snapped up by one of the big two, as they are in a position to increase their wages, even if they don't end up getting much playing time! As a result the Old Firm aren't well loved by those of us who support provincial teams. Of course, one could add some other reasons...

It is difficult to select one game after a lifetime of highlights (and lowlights) but here's one of the games that has loomed large in my memory. It took place on May 12 2007. A crucial match at the end of the season where St Mirren simply had to win to avoid relegation from the Premier League. There was no trophy at stake here – instead it was the very survival of the team in Scotland's top division that was in question. St Mirren were playing Motherwell, away from home, and at halftime the 'Steelmen' were a goal to the good. Then early in the second half they were awarded a penalty, which they duly converted. Now we were 2–0 down and not even a draw could save us. We needed to score three goals. Time was running out for Saints.

Then on came two subs, strikers Billy Mehmet and John Sutton. After a few minutes Sutton scored, when a downward header at goal went through the legs of the Motherwell goalkeeper. It was a fortunate goal, but there was nothing lucky about the ball coolly and expertly placed into the net by Mehmet just four minutes later. St Mirren were level!

Then, on 83 minutes, as the clock continued to run down and St Mirren continued to press the Motherwell goal, the ball broke free to Sutton at the edge of the box. There were a ruck of players between him and the goal. All around me people screamed "Hit it John!" and the big striker volleyed the ball between the players and into the roof of the net.

At this point I found myself in the air with the normal rules of gravity in temporary suspension along with the other Saints fans directly behind the goal. As the bodies jumped we seemed to be wedged together for a few seconds before beginning our descent to land in the seats below us. The TV commentator, realising the enormity of the occasion, was reduced to speaking in theological terms. "St Mirren have come back from the dead!" he announced excitedly.

In his book *Fever Pitch,* author Nick Hornby made the point that the fan really is the true heart of any club. Players, managers and board members may come and go and sign for other teams, but the fan is there permanently. In other words, the (mostly anonymous) fans care much more about their team than even the most famous of players. Players and managers may move on for more money, or perceived career advancement but the fans are there for the long haul.

Once I saw a very short TV interview with Tony Fitzpatrick, the legendary former player who had come to the end of his second spell as manager. He wanted to thank the players for their work and support and so they held an event. They all went out together for a fish tea! That was all he said. I immediately thought of the big clubs like the Old Firm who would be regularly jetting off to training camps in the sunshine of Spain or playing prestige tournaments in the USA. And here were St Mirren celebrating with a fish supper in Paisley.

David McLachlan *is Minister of Langside Parish Church, and a writer and broadcaster*

Chapter 8

The Oddly Paved Path to Dumbarton

Simon Barrow

Football is a leap of faith, without doubt. Or perhaps, like many acts of daring, it is what turns out to be a life full of reasons to doubt, but one so bathed in the electricity of passion that its more troubling provocations are held almost permanently at bay.

My own dive into the football dark side began early in life. When I was around eight years of age, in fact – and then again in the oddly paved journey to becoming a Dumbarton supporter (of all things!) three years later. Coming from a largely non-sporting family, and with few natural athletic abilities myself, I still cannot fully explain how football first grabbed my soul. But when the strange grip took hold, it proved immovable.

My earliest fully conscious remembrance of the game – other than as a kick-about with a tennis ball in the playground at school, or playing in the backyard with friends across the road in the posh southern English suburb where I grew up – was the 1966 World Cup Final between England and West Germany at Wembley on 30th July 1966. Scottish fans of a delicate disposition might feel inclined to avert their eyes at this point, but let me assure you – this story (unlike that particular game, for many Scots) ended well.

In the build-up to the Final there had been much to-do at the preparatory school I attended in leafy Kew Gardens. (See? I told you it was posh.) Flags, bunting, songs ... we endured the whole works. There was a German kid in the class ahead of me, which was not commonplace in a largely mono-cultural, über middle class southern English community back then. I cannot actually remember his name these days. Nor can I pretend that we were particularly close at the time. But I do recall feeling rather sorry for him, and finding the atmosphere of enforced In-ger-land patriotism annoying and suffocating.

That sense of irritation grew exponentially as the Great Day approached. Watching the World Cup Final and cheering on England was compulsory, it seemed. Not for me. A lifetime of rebellion was launched on that hot summer afternoon in 1966, as I announced to my parents that I really didn't care if "we" won or not. In fact, I'd be pleased for my German friend (I'd decided that he needed elevating in status for the purposes of this argument) if West Germany triumphed. This monumental treachery to the land of my birth was not welcome, to say the least. I was told that if I was going to be childish, I would jolly well have to sit on the floor, while the kids from across the road (who were older than me) could deport themselves on the sofa with the adults.

This was a humiliation too far. I announced that I was going outside to play football instead. So I took up my ball and walked. While everyone else in the household watched England beat West Germany 4–2, propelled to victory by a goal from Geoff Hurst that science has proved never fully crossed the line (in case you are still wondering), young Simon was downstairs kicking a ball against a wall and hoping the Germans would win. As so often in my football life, it was not to be.

Having embarked upon a reckless path of betraying my country through football before I was even out of short trousers, the strong interest I had in the game had to turn somewhere. But the path to Boghead Park was still a rather crooked one. First, in 1967, Scotland gloriously beat England 3–2 at Wembley in the old British Home Championship, pronouncing themselves World Champions over the auld enemy. And there I was, watching the game eagerly on television, cheering Scotland on, to my father's puzzlement.

The reasoning here, if such it can be called, was two-fold. First, I had already lit upon Denis Law as my boyhood football hero. I can't remember exactly how that happened, but one of my proudest possessions to this day is a signed picture of the Lawman producing a magical 'bicycle kick' to score against Spurs in the FA Cup. Incredibly, the goal was disallowed, because sometimes the rules of the game have no sense of historical justice.

Anyway, I digress. Law was playing for Scotland, and indeed grabbed a typically cheeky goal in that unexpected Wembley triumph. I was overjoyed. My mother, too, was quietly pleased the Scots were doing well. For whereas my father (though he lacked more than a passing interest in sport) was quintessentially an Englander in both instinct and affiliation, my mother was one of those confirmedly middle-class English ladies who loved all things Scottish. By which I mean she revelled in the cultural clichés of tartan, bagpipes and lochs – while never, to my knowledge, visiting the country once in her entire life.

In short, I was mostly lured into life-long support for Scotland and Scottish football by Denis Law and my mother's penchant for shortbread. I finally moved north of the border 43 years later, and the rest is history. Well, almost. I haven't got to the crucial Dumbarton bit yet. That further fit of madness came a little over two years on ... bear with me. My interest in Scottish football had, in the meantime, been further cemented by watching Celtic's Lisbon Lions bring home the European Cup (25th May 1967) on a battered black-and-white telly, and then deeply mourning the absence through injury of Denis Law as Manchester United clobbered Benfica 4–1 in the final of the same competition the following year.

Between these footballing monuments my grandfather had taken me and a school friend, Guy Pilkington, to watch his beloved Brentford beat Notts County 2–1 at Griffin Park on 14 October 1967. (The scorers were Edwards and Lawther, in case you were wondering, and the irascible Scot Jimmy Sirrell was on the home bench.) That live game changed my life further. I still remember the bustle of the crowd, the clatter of rattles (this was five decades ago) and the sickly sweet smell of pipe smoke on the terrace. I loved it. Logically, I should be a Brentford supporter these days. But as we have already established, logic has little to do with the Beautiful Game. I used by then to watch the Scottish football results on TV at just after five o'clock on a Saturday afternoon, because I liked the names of the teams. Queen of the South and Partick Thistle sounded a bit more exotic to my youthful ears than Scunthorpe or Workington, perhaps.

So it was that on the fateful day of 13 December 1969 that Dumbarton lost miserably, conceding six goals away to Stranraer ... and eleven year-old Simon Barrow, watching the score roll down the TV screen, announced to his parents that he was now a Sons fans. (Well, he would have put it that way, if he'd known that their nickname was the Sons of the Rock at that point.) Being sensible people my parents instantly pointed out that I had no connection to Dumbarton whatsoever. The nearest family link to Scotland was that my maternal great grandmother had spent some time in Ayrshire, apparently. Which is miles away.

Anyway, such pleading made no difference. I was a Dumbarton supporter, I had decided, and the offbeat obsession – which seems quite normal now – continued until I was able to attend my first game at Boghead as a student. The Sons lost, of course. In fact it was some nine games until I actually saw us score a goal. That was against Hamilton Accies in 1987, in a match we also lost. The fans on the terrace must have been wondering why this unhinged Sassenach was going crazy over a goal that made no difference to the outcome (we eventually went down 2–1), and had every right to do so. But for me it is still a landmark moment.

To skip a good deal of the agony filling the thirty-two years since that goal was scored, here I am today, in 2019: a season ticket holder at Dumbarton for ten years, the contributor of a regular column in the *Sons View* programme for twelve years, and someone who has a mere round-trip of 120 miles from Edinburgh for a home game – which definitely compares favourably to the 650+ for travelling from down south.

For goodness' sake, I've even been the unpaid Press Officer for the club, as well as an activist in the Sons Supporters' Trust, and founding co-chair of the Scottish Football Supporters Association. The strange football faith still runs deep, you could say, and doubts about the craziness of the game are mostly not to do with the Sons – though we have our trials and tribulations, for sure – but with billionaire-dominated Corporate Football. That has brought resources tumbling in (for the few, not the many) in recent years, but has also drained away much romance and loyalty from the game in the twenty-first century.

As footnote to this strange tale of how football really is (beyond) belief, I should add that on my fiftieth birthday I discovered that two of my late father's closest friends, after I left home, actually came from Dumbarton – and he never told me, even though he knew I supported the team. Incredible. That's how disconnected you can be from the game, if football fortune bypasses you so cruelly. The tale by which I made that discovery, incidentally, involves the Internet, Amnesty International, Burma and a lovely chap (and fellow English Sons fan) called Tim Rhead. But it can wait for another day...

Simon Barrow *is a writer and think-tank director. He is a pacifist member of the Tartan Army. He lives in Edinburgh*

Chapter 9

Cows and Beef *

Ron Ferguson

So Senga is entertaining her lover, Jock, in her 20-storey flat in Glasgow. Suddenly, the sound of approaching feet is heard – probably Senga's husband. Like a man possessed, Jock springs to his feet, exits through the open window and dangles from the window sill. He cannot maintain his grip, though. As he hits the ground, dead, a letter comes through Senga's door. The postman.

Hearing sounds of distress, Senga's neighbour and best friend, Avril, rushes in. The hyperventilating Senga recounts the terrible events. Ever helpful, Avril asks if there's anything she can do. Senga has a flash of inspiration. "Run downstairs and put a shammy in Jock's hand," she shouts.

This charming tale came to my mind a while ago when I was in a BBC Radio Scotland studio in Glasgow. I was taking part in a live broadcast of the Off the Ball football programme, which is hosted by Stuart Cosgrove and Tam Cowan, the self-described "odd couple" of Scottish football. The programme is labelled "the most petty and ill-informed football show on radio".

Anyway, Tam Cowan had just been informing his large audience about my presence in the studio. "We have a man of the cloth with us," he shouted, then added, "he's a window cleaner". As a regular listener to the scurrilous fitba programme that sends up its guests, I knew to expect some irreverent badinage. Maybe a foolhardy thing for a minister to do. Why was I putting myself through it? Well, I was launching a book about football. (In the old days, the writer's job was to write the book and deliver the manuscript on time; nowadays, the writer is also expected to sell the book.) But I was also there because I enjoy Stuart and Tam's take on the Scottish game.

They have a soft spot for supporters of lower league football clubs, who follow their unfashionable teams up and down the country in good times and bad. The duo are no respecters of persons or reputations. They are not in thrall to the Old Firm of Rangers and Celtic. They are genuine football fans - Stuart supports St Johnstone and Tam

Motherwell – who care about the Scottish game. As the two-hour show progressed, I saw at first hand just how outstanding professionals they are – winging it with quick-witted banter.

My dad used to take me to Central Park, Cowdenbeath, when I was a child. He was a regular attender. When he and my mother honeymooned in the Hillfoots, near the Ochil hills, it just so happened that Alloa were at home to Cowdenbeath. My doughty grandfather, Alex Ferguson, patriarch, painter and Kirk elder, was rarely missing from his seat in the Central Park stand, tartan rug over his knees. My great grand aunt, Margaret Pollock, an antiques dealer who brought the first leather football to Cowdenbeath in June 1880 can lay claim to being the true founder of Cowdenbeath FC (which was formed seven years before Celtic FC). I was reared not just on stories of the legendary Cowden players of earlier days, but on tales of mining disasters, and the struggles of West Fife miners to get better wages. My third cousin, the great Jennie Lee, honed her rhetorical skills in the streets of Cowdenbeath during the miners' strikes.

Coal and football and Cowdenbeath are in my bodymind. Mad Cowdenbeath Disease, which attacks the brain, and to which there is no known antidote, has travelled down the generations through my children - Fiona, Neil and Ally - and my grandchildren, Olly and Dan.

After I had completed a biography of George MacLeod, founder of the Iona Community, for Harper Collins in 1990, I decided to write about my home team, set against the rise and decline of the coal mining industry. I was minister of St Magnus Cathedral, Kirkwall, at the time. Of the books I have written, the semi-autobiographical *Black Diamonds and the Blue Brazil* was the most fun to write. When it was published by Bill Williams of Famedram in 1993, it was barely noticed. Then, curiously, it began to flourish by word of mouth. It was picked up by some of the heavyweight London papers, and was soon routinely described as a "best-selling cult book".

Most football books of that era were about the big, glamorous clubs, or were ghost-written celebrity memoirs. A book about the ups and downs of one of the least successful football clubs in Britain was a curiosity. I was asked to speak about the book at a convention of European football supporters in the South Bank, London, along with Jim Baxter, a fellow pupil of Beath High school.

Black Diamonds has been out of print for a couple of years, but there is still steady demand for it. The new book is a completely updated 21st anniversary edition with additional chapters, plus an introduction by

Sir Alex Ferguson, and forewords by Craig Brown, Jim Leishman and poet-theologian Kathy Galloway (who doesn't like football). As well as being about fitba, it's about journalism, politics, religion, tragedy and community spirit.

Bringing the story up to date reminded me of how much more fun there is in lower league football. Cowdenbeath had an Egyptian forward called Tewfick Abdullah, who was called after a local greyhound. (The greyhound was slow.) In more recent times, we had a mad 42-year-old goalkeeper called John Martin. When a game was a bit boring, the Cowden fans would sing, "Johnny, Johnny swing on the bar"; the custodian would swing back and forward on the crossbar, toothless grin on his face.

We also had a French European food mountain from Coatbridge, Armand Oné. When the Cowden faithful chanted, "Oné, Oné, Oné, Pizza Hut, Pizza Hut, Pizza Hut," the lumbering striker would dance on the pitch. Cowden manager Craig Levein once persuaded his friend, Pasquale Bruno, the ex-Juventus and Hearts star, to make a cameo appearance for the Blue Brazil in a match at Central Park against Ross County. The tanned Italian superstar strolled elegantly around the Fife Maracana. Then, with Cowden 2–0 ahead, Stuart Juner, a Cowden terracing wit, shouted: "Hey Pasquale, where have you been all my life?" Bruno looked up and grinned - and completely missed the ball, allowing the Ross County striker to run straight through and score. The Blue Brazil ended up losing 3–2.

You don't get that kind of fun at Ibrox or Parkhead. They take themselves awfy seriously there. If Rangers or Celtic lose a game, some fans become suicidal; if Blue Brazil fans were to be suicidal every time they lost a game, West Fife would be depopulated. At one time Cowden failed to win at home in the league for 18 months; things were so bad that I was summoned down to Central Park to perform the footballing equivalent of an exorcism.

It's not so long ago since Fergus McCann and David Murray said that smaller clubs should disappear from the Scottish leagues. In fact, Cowdenbeath's youth system was giving local youngsters good coaching at a time when Rangers and Celtic were concentrating on signing foreign dumplings at considerable expense.

In July 2013, Scottish football was reorganised (once again). Cowdenbeath found themselves in the Scottish Championship, the second most senior division in Scottish football. The Blue Brazil would be playing teams such as Rangers, Hearts, and Hibs. Our dynamic strike force of Greg Stewart (spotted by a Cowden scout while playing amateur football) and Kane Hemmings (a Rangers cast-off) were virtually unplayable. Securing our place in the Championship by beating the auld enemy Dunfermline Athletic 3–0 at East End Park on the final day of the play-offs was one of the best days of my life (equalled only by the day I turned out as a substitute for Cowdenbeath in a pre-season friendly) Stewart and Hemmings were snapped up by Dundee, and then moved south for big bucks. Were Cowdenbeath FC rewarded for coaching young players? Of course not.

2018: Orkney is a long way from Cowdenbeath, but I've bought my season ticket once again. I know there will be more disappointments than moments of bliss. As in life? Can Cows and Beef continue to defy football gravity indefinitely? Pass me the shammy. Or even the chamois. Remember, I'm a man of the cloth.

Ron Ferguson is a journalist, former leader of the Iona Community and author of Black Diamonds and the Blue Brazil

* The reference to Cows and Beef (!) is that when Ron was minister of St Magnus Cathedral, the children couldn't understand why he followed a team so called! [Editor]

Chapter 10

Ah've Never Had a Killie Pie

Ailsa Henderson

Noo let me say richt at the stert
Tho ah support them frae the hert
An tho ah'm 'Killie till I die'
Ah've never had a Killie pie!
An ah've been gaun tae Rugby Park
Sometimes in daylicht, sometimes dark
For gaun on fifty-seeven years
At times wi pleisure, times wi tears.
Times we went hame broken-hertit,
Times disaster wis avertit,
Times the luck seemed quite unnervin,
Times we won wi'oot deservin!
Times we aa sang 'Paper Roses'
(Tho' whaur that came frae naebody 'knowses'!)
Times when on the ither haun
The man ahint us in the Staun
Because the gemme wis awfy dreich
Wid tell his neebour 'this is keich'
'C'mon we'll hiv a brek-in Shug,
You go first, ah'll bring the dug'.

But back tae when it aa began –
It never wis a conscious plan –
It wid be nineteen sixty – August –
Ma faither, sittin at his tea just
The week afore the season stertit,
Remarked ma brither had depairtit
Awa tae Glesca there tae study
An that left faither wi nae buddy
Tae gang wi him tae watch the gemme
So ah said 'That's aw richt, ah'll come'.

An that wis it – fae that day on
The die wis cast, the seed wis sown
An life wid never be the same
Fur ah wis hooked on the beautiful game.
Ah've mind ma first gemme – if ah'm richt –
Against the Hearts? – a Wednesday nicht?
But naw ma memory's played a trick
Kilmarnock Standard's records pick
Oot Celtic as the opposition
The opening gemme o ma first season.
But ah wis richt – it wis a draw
A guid gemme tae, we baith scored twa.
Sae mony things ah had tae learn!
It wisnae easy tae discern
Whit wis a 'corner' or a 'shy'
An often ah wad wunner why
The referee had blawn his whustle
Until ma faither muttered 'This'll
mebbe stop that blatant foulin!
While aa the time the crowd wis howlin!
The followin year the League Cup draw
Brocht the highest score ah ever saw:
"Along the line the train came puffin
Kilmarnock aicht an Airdrie nuffin.'"
An on an on we went that year –
Tae Hampden! Wi that trophy near
As dammit, in oor very paw
We cuidnae score, we let in twa!
Sae sadly we wis left wi nuffin
That Rangers team gied us a stuffin.
Back then on terracin we stood
In winter coat an scarf an hood
In rain an snaw an ice an frost
As Killie won, or drew, or lost
Until, ma faither got his pension
An telt me it wis his intention
That him an me fae that day on
Wid sit in comfort in the Staun.
(An no he hadnae lost his reason
My Christmas present wid be ma Season).

An sae the seasons came an went
An happy Setterdays wis spent
Watchin Killie's laichs an highs
Mixin cheers wi groans an sighs.
Ma favourite players, ower mony a year
Some o them lang gone noo ah fear
Frae Bertie Black, a Cumnock man
Tae Pascali, the Italian
Ray Montgomerie, an 'Big D'
The half-back line o Clark(e) x 3
Solid defensive at the back
But no bad either in attack.
Frank Beattie weel whit can ah say
The yin-club-man's inspiring play -
Wi' sic a captain – wha could bate us?
Nae wunner he has legend status!
Wee Tommy, Davie Provan tae
An 'Caspar' Smith an 'Hooky' Hay
Ah still can mind as clear as day
Yin goal that Caspar pit away.
He took a corner – it flew – it birled
In at the 'postage stamp' it curled
Hoo he did it? ah'll never ken
(Peety he never did it again!)

An ah wis sad tae say 'Adieux'
Tae 'Freddie-long-legs' Dindeleux
Wha served us weel, an noo his name
Is in the Killie 'Hall of Fame'
An Eremenko – no the quickest
But his passin wis the slickest
There never wis a better signin
Made by Mixu Patalainen.

Oor greatest moments spanned decades
The memory o them never fades
The first - for me - that glorious day
When we were playin Hearts - away

Hopin, at last, the 'League' tae win –
Oor chances could be seen as thin,
It shuirly wis 'High Noon' for Killie
(The manager then wis Waddell – Wullie)
That last gemme – April '65
When Sneddon scored, kep hope alive
We had tae win by twae clear goals
An aa the players had their roles
Like McIlroy, wha as required
Gied us the margin we desired!
But still there wis an hour tae go
would we make it? Would we no!
Fur goalie Ferguson's great savin'
Wad send us Killie fans hame ravin!
While Hearts were left to rue the day
As doon in saicont place they'd stay.
Oh whit a day an whit a team an
Efter five lang years o dreamin
Five years o bein' runners-up –
We'd finally made it tae the tap.

(An mind, that year, the 'Auld Firm' greats
could only manage fifth an eighth!)

A lang time passes – a different tale
I think we hae to draw a veil
For efter enjoying 'golden years'
In Europe, Killie disappears
Doun the divisions, until by turns
An a bit o help fae Tommy Burns –
An the efforts o the Fleeting brithers
Began tae pou us back thegither.

Things chynge an sae we sclimm back up
An reach the final o the Cup –
Anither chance for glory given
In Mey o' 1997:
Tho Falkirk put up quite a fight
It's thanks tae Paul – we got it 'Wright'!

For we were made o sterner stuff
An Paul's yin goal wis juist enough.
A triumph ne'er tae be forgotten
(Felt a wee bit sorry for Alec Totten).
In 2012 anither try
Tae win the League Cup cam oor wey
As underdugs at Hampden then
We scarcely could believe it when
Tae bate the Celtic aa it needit
Wis the single goal van Tornhout heidit.

Afore ah stop, jist ae thing mair
Ah'm sorry faither wisnae there
But there wis nae pynt in greetin
He had tae gang tae a Session meetin
And thus he missed in late September
That gemme, ah yet can weel remember...
The legendary Eintracht gemme
We stertit three nil doon tae them
An lost anither early on
The hale crowd jist let oot a groan
Whit noo? we've shuirly lost oor chance –
But then began the merry dance
When oor five goals went rattlin in.
McFadzean playin oot his skin
Contributed goal nummer three
(By that time we were on a spree)
For McIlroy had scored afore him
'C'mon, C'mon', the crowd wis roarin
Till cam the goal by McInally
That brocht tae fower Kilmarnock's tally.

Then Hamilton, wha'd scored the first,
Raised the excitement fit tae burst
When just afore the whustle blew –
He got his tally up tae two.
An then the brek-in really happened
Amongst the shoutin, cheerin, clappin,
For we had won the tie five - fower
It wis Kilmarnock's finest hour.

An noo ma tale is aa but finished
Ma team thae days, faur fae diminished,
Are playin weel an daein fine
It's clear tae see – they 'toe the line'
For Stephen Clarke an Alex Dyer:
As they continue tae inspire,
There's only yin thing left worth sayin –
'Here's tae them, lang may they reign!
An so may ah be spared tae see
Ah wheen mair gemmes afore ah dee!
Some wins – tae keep the fans aboot
The Premiership? Ah hae ma doots
Anither Cup? Ye never know!
But yin thing's shuir – we'll huv a go -
At challengin the rich and famous
Fur mind – oor motto's 'Confidemus!'

Ailsa Henderson *has worked with Oxfam and Christian Aid*

Chapter 11

Rose Reilly: Keeping Faith in the Women's Game

Gerry Hassan

Scottish football is on the way up – at the international level, in quality, achievements and in its recognition by others. Our national team has just beaten the mighty Brazil for the first time ever, and if that were not enough, has qualified after a long fallow period for the World Cup finals taking place in summer 2019 in France.

It has been a long and difficult journey to get to this. Previously the Scottish women's game was marginalised, patronised, dismissed, and even, the subject of banning for much of the 20th century, which denied at least two generations of talented women the opportunity to play football at a senior level in this country.

All this forms a backdrop to the timely, moving new film about the life and achievements of Rose Reilly, made by Purple TV and Margot McCuaig, and which was first broadcast on BBC Alba. It tells how Reilly overcame entrenched resistance from football authorities in Scotland, and found fame and fortune in Italy playing for AC Milan, winning the Women's World Cup with Italy in 1984, and the same year being awarded the accolade of Women's World Player of the Year.

Her personal story provides the opportunity to bring to public attention the long forgotten Neanderthal attitudes of those who ran football in this country and saw it as the preserve of men, with the women's game as something to be discouraged and actively suppressed.

Women's football was formally banned in Scotland in 1921 in the aftermath of the First World War (it also being banned in England that year). This was a conscious attempt after war, and intensive female employment in industry, to re-emphasise traditional female roles in the home which football was seen to undermine.

For those who think such prehistoric attitudes lie deep in Scotland's distant past prepare for a shock. In 1971 UEFA decided that the time had now come to promote and integrate women's football and passed a near-unanimous vote to this effect – 31 votes to one – the single dissenting voice being the dinosaurs of the SFA. And it was to take until 1974 for the football authorities to finally relent and unban the women's game here, the SFA's official minutes recording that "they reluctantly gave official recognition to the women's game", waiting until 1998 before they brought the game under the auspices of the SFA.

This is the context of Rose Reilly's life story, achievements and many successes – gained in the face of entrenched and unenlightened attitudes on the part of senior men in positions of power running the game in Scotland.

Born in Stewarton, Ayrshire, in 1955, into a working class and Catholic family where she was one of eight, Reilly knew from an early age that she was gifted and loved football. At the tender age of four, she had a crisis of identity when she was given a doll as a Christmas present, which appalled her. "I went straight out among the local kids," she remembers, "and eventually managed to swap that doll for a football."

This was not the end of things but only the beginning. "My mother didn't know what to do with me," says Rose, who showed her identification and love for the game by sleeping each night with her football for a whole year – "I fell in love with it. I was scared my mother or one of my brothers would take it off me."

In her pre-pubescent years, Rose managed to play football in boy's teams by cutting her hair very short to look like a boy and calling herself Ross. Playing in the boy's game brought her success and attention, aided by her pace and growing ability, but this was to bring her first major disappointment.

After a particularly successful game in the boy's team where she scored a barrel load of goals, word got around of the young player's prowess. This led to the interest of a Celtic FC scout who said to the club, "I'd like to sign right away yer wee number seven." To which the youth coach replied, "Sorry, you can't, that's actually a wee lassie." Rose remembers this defining moment well – "I got talking to that scout and I was raging about it. I just couldn't understand why I couldn't play for Celtic."

Reilly continued to play boy's football until puberty and biology made it obvious to all that she was a girl. This brought with it the weight of disapproval from school and church authorities in nearby Kilmarnock. "They finally got exasperated with me," comments Rose, "and I got the belt, right across the hands. The headmaster said to me, 'You are never going to learn, are you?' I said, 'Naw, it's youse that are never going to learn. I just want to play football, I'm doing nothing wrong." Reilly adds poignantly: "Back then sometimes I felt like I would be burnt at the stake for playing football."

Reilly as a young woman not only showed great aptitude as a footballer, but also in athletics, where she could have represented Scotland. But it was football to which her heart, commitment and skill belonged. Yet in 1970s Scotland the football authorities were doing all they could to discourage the women's game, forcing talented players like Reilly to seek opportunity elsewhere.

She moved to France as a teenager in 1972, signing for Stade de Reims, before the following year taking the big step of moving to Italy and signing for AC Milan and playing at the legendary San Siro. This was to be the making of Reilly as she played seventeen years in Italian football, including for Lecce and Trani, winning eight league titles, four cups, and twice the Golden Boot for the most goals in a single season, scoring an outstanding 43 and 45 goals respectively.

Reilly's years in Italy were among the happiest in her life. "I totally embraced Italy," she recalls, talking of how she loved everything about the culture, from the cafes to nightlife, fashion and style. "I started drinking espresso coffee. My motto was, when in Rome, do as the Romans do. I was being wined and dined in restaurants all over Italy. Previously, the only place I'd been to was the chippie in Stewarton."

Not only did Reilly perform at club level in one of the most passionate football countries in the world, but she also established herself at international level. Not for Scotland, but for Italy, with Reilly as the captain of the Italian team lifting the World Cup in 1984, scoring one of her team's three goals in their 3–1 defeat of West Germany.

This is an uplifting, life-affirming story, about the triumph of talent, passion and belief rising above the small-minded and petty bureaucrats who ran men's football, wanted to keep it as a closed shop and to keep women permanently outside of it.

Reilly is a wonderful character and witness to her own story and her achievements. She tells her account with wit, humour and a sense of authenticity which goes to her core. This is a woman who has encountered, what would have been to most people, insurmountable barriers and prejudice – and defeated them. When asked if she still feels anger towards those who banned her from football in her own country, she displays a Zen-like attitude with a soft degree of incredulity that people running the game could have been so stupid, along with a charm and great line in self-depreciation that belies deep courage and resilience.

Eventually the football authorities caught up. In 2007 Reilly was at long last inducted into the Football Hall of Fame, despite the disapproval and opposition of some of football's dinosaurs. And this week Reilly and some of her fellow pioneers have been awarded in retrospect national caps for international games, before the SFA unbanned the game.

Reilly's role as a trailblazer and ambassador is now widely recognised across the game, although unreconstructed male chauvinists still linger in parts of the football world. The Scottish coach of the women's team heading off to France, Shelley Kerr, openly talks of the inspiration and pioneering role of Reilly (and her team mates Edna Neillis and Elsie Cook) all those years ago in what seem now like dark ages.

Rose Reilly's accomplishments – as a player, as a role model and as someone aiding social change – is unquestionable and more than that, humbling and empowering, given the obstacles she faced from her earliest years. It is accurate, and right, to call her one of Scotland's true football giants and legends – someone who should be seen and spoken of in the same breath as household names like Billy McNeill, John Greig, Archie Gemmell and Jimmy Johnstone, to name a few.

The film of her life, 'Rose Reilly', covers her story from her earliest years in Stewarton to the present, where at the age of 64 she reflects on a life that included retiring from football at the age of 40; marriage to an Argentinian doctor and psychotherapist, Norberto Peralta, and at 45, the birth of her only daughter, Valentina, who is now 19.

This is a story that needed to be told – about more than just football and the success of one extraordinary woman. It is also about the oppressive society Scotland was not that long ago, and how we all owe a debt of gratitude to the likes of Rose Reilly for refusing to defer to the mediocre men who said 'no, you cannae dae that'.

But it also one where we should not imagine that the sexists and misogynists have been completely defeated – think in recent years of Tam Cowan's dismissive remarks on women's football; or that the accomplishments of Reilly and others have now been universally recognised – with no entry for Reilly or anyone else associated with women's football in the just published New Biographical Dictionary of Scottish Women. It is wonderful that the women's game is now being celebrated, but we still have a lot of progress to catch up on, and across society we are far removed from gender equality in any walk of life.

A special word has to go to Margot McCuaig who championed this as a project and saw it into production. "Making this film has been an emotional journey, but also an empowering one," says Margot. Rose's "legacy of self-belief, determination and hard-fought for success against the backdrop of deep-rooted misogyny in sport and society will undoubtedly inspire generations to come."

It was appropriate then that as the successful Scottish national women's team played their last match at Hampden against Jamaica before going to the World Cup in France that the SFA finally acknowledged the success of Rose and a generation of other women pioneers. At long last they have decided to recognise Rose and the team who played the international against England in 1972 – before the game was unbanned.

Gerry Hassan *is a Dundee United fan, and regularly follows junior football across Scotland. He is a writer and commentator on Scottish politics, society and culture*

Chapter 12

Tales of the Tartan Army

Iain Whyte

As one who was brought up in London, along with many exiles, my chance to see Scotland play in my early days was limited to the biennial Wembley game. Few can have seen a Scottish goal within 60 seconds of their first experience of the national team, but Tommy Ring of Clyde achieved that in 1957. We still lost 2–1 to goals by Derek Kevan and Duncan Edwards. But Willie Fernie of Celtic had an equaliser chalked off by the Referee, Piet Roomer from the Netherlands, and I still find it hard to forgive him! I did see a victory in 1963, the year that Jim Baxter made his debut and scored twice.

The luckiest escape ever was after my father obtained two tickets for the 1961 game. At a student conference I had fallen madly in love with a girl from Plymouth, and the thought of her company was an even greater attraction than Wembley. My father took a friend and saw the 9–3 debacle that led to the transportation to Australia of the hapless Celtic and Scotland goalkeeper Frank Haffey.

During a spell of teaching in Falkirk Technical College I was roasted by some very difficult youngsters in the Vehicle Body Building section, whose enthusiasm for attending a General Studies class between 5.30pm and 7.00pm was not conspicuous. I was moved when, learning of my passion for the beautiful game, the chief troublemaker, who had been to another Wembley disaster (5–1), handed me a crumpled programme at the following week's class. I offered to pay him. "Naw, sur," he said with a grin. "Ah knocked it aff an Englishman." That was the game where a lone tammied Scot was reputed to have waved a bottle at the departing English fans and declared triumphantly "You'se couldna' score six!"

A foreign venture with the Tartan Army is always full of the unexpected. In June 1997. I set off with my son David and a Russian-speaking friend for Belarus. We flew to Warsaw and then took the overnight Moscow train to Minsk. I had been warned that at the Polish border the carriages were jacked up and the wheels changed by hand to fit the old Tsarist guage in Russia. The Tartan Army were mainly unaware of this, and at 2.00am, sustained by countless cans of Tennent's lager, many believed that they were hallucinating or going to heaven.

We stayed in the same hotel as the Scottish team – ludicrously cheap and fairly comfortable. They had the top floor but took the only lift. David told me that he had shared it with 'the man who broke my heart at Wembley.' (Gary McAlister's penalty miss in the 1996 Euros). I travelled on match day in the lift with Darren Jackson and wished him luck. "One goal will do," said I cheerfully. He nodded. After a lifeless and goalless first half, Jackson went over in the box and McAlister converted the spot-kick.

In those days the SFA provided a full time guide, helper, and friend for the Tartan Army. Marjorie Nimmo, a former teacher in Lanarkshire, was mother to us all, and how she kept on smiling throughout the inevitable crises I'll never know. At one point she was armed with an enormous bag of liquorice allsorts, which she generously proceeded to pass round. I questioned the wisdom of this by asking Marjorie what made her think that any Scotland supporter needed a laxative. When a fan arrived ten minutes into the game in Prague, having excessively enjoyed the excellent and cheap Czech beer, and asked the score, I gave him a fright by pretending we were two down. Marjorie immediately came to his rescue. "You're a minister, Iain," she said sternly. "You shouldna' be telling lies."

The minister identity crept out into these travels. However it was an article by Kevin McAllion and a photo in the *Sunday Mail* captioned 'Tartan Army Chaplain is praying for the jersey' that brought a new dimension to my pilgrimages. Only once had there been anything official, when the Church of Sweden asked for volunteer Chaplains at the Euros in 1992 and Erik Cramb and Tom Gordon (authors of pieces in this book) had gone over there. But in Dortmund, and in Prague I was greeted as "the big man of God," recognisable from the paper.

Interesting brief conversations took place, but in the King Baodouin stadium in Brussels it became serious. A giant of a man turned to me, after we had done the all too familiar exercise of turning unlikely victory into tragic defeat. 'Hey Big Man' said this punter ominously, who towered over me. 'Ah spent two hours praying in the Cathedral. And it hasna' done any good.' 'Why are you telling me?' I asked weakly. 'Because,' he growled, 'ah know who you are.' I suddenly had an image of Ricky Fulton's Rev I M Jolly sharing a cell in Barlinnie with a man charged with GBH on a Church of Scotland minister and demanding to have his confession heard!

The Belarus trip qualified for a ticket to the World Cup opener against Brazil in 1998. To say the atmosphere was electric would be a gross understatement. Paris was a huge party, and the goodwill of the Brazilian fans and their sympathetic buying of drinks for us after the game did something to dull the disappointment of narrow defeat. When John Collins equalised with a penalty, the crowd erupted into song, "Who put the ball in the Brazilian net ... Johnnie, O Johnnie." A young woman in front of me burst into tears. In my best pastoral mode I comforted her with the words "Don't worry, it won't last." It didn't for more than several minutes, when the hapless Tom Boyd scored an own goal. On reflection, I think she had second sight.

Having watched the Ghana national team when I was a Youth Worker for the church there, I have taken many an African visitor to see Scotland play. In 1973, as International Chaplain in Glasgow, I gathered a motley crew to the terraces for the vital World Cup qualifier against the then Czechoslovakia. When Jo Jordan's header secured us a place in the first World Cup Finals we had seen in 16 years, Hampden erupted. For five minutes I searched the crowd for my guests. Eventually he, a Methodist teacher from Zimbabwe and a strict teetotaler, emerged with a grin and a bottle of half- full Buckfast. "It was the only way to stop someone hugging me," he said. "He insisted I shared his celebrations." Much later I took a South African friend to see an unlikely draw against Italy. Even in a now all seated stadium, the portly man behind us got so excited by our goal that he flew through the air and landed on Sam. Fortunately there was a good deal of bulk on my friend and he emerged full of goodwill and none the worse.

In the Millennium year, Tam Cowan and Stuart Cosgrove in the gut wrenching and irreverent programme, *Off the Ball,* interviewed me on my 60th birthday, and just before another Scotland slump against a Baltic team. I was determined not to succumb to their overwhelming banter, and told a long story of a fundraising game for Christian Aid which I organized and played in, against Scottish ex-internationals at St Mirren Park when I was a minister in Paisley. I described in graphic detail challenging the bulky John Hughes of Celtic – 'Yogi bear' – for a ball in the air, and substituting Alex Ferguson, when he pulled a hamstring, Tam said breathlessly, "Reverend, we're going to have to stop you there. We've run out of time."

Why do we do it? How can we continue to have faith, let alone hope, in a national team that with terrible regularity snatches, as the late

Ian Archer put it, "defeat from the jaws of victory." As I write this, a further humiliation has just come in from Kazakhstan in Central Asia to which 650 Tartan Army pilgrims made the trek. Although we don't recognise it, we humans, almost as much as animals, are creatures of habit. And there is a masochistic streak in us all. Add to that mix the Calvinist parody that is deep in our psyche, that enjoyment is not for the righteous and punishment is always deserved, and we perhaps come closer to answering the question. In the end I prefer the words of that ancient writer of a letter to the Hebrew church. "Faith is the substance of things hoped for, the evidence of things not seen." Or as the great Sir Kenny Dalglish might say, "mebbes aye, mebbes naw."

Iain Whyte has been Chaplain to the Universities of St Andrews and Edinburgh, a parish minister, a youth worker in Ghana, and Head of Christian Aid Scotland

Chapter 13

Confessions of a Theologian and Jambo

David Fergusson

I begin with this confession (now that I'm a Hearts supporter) – I grew up a Rangers' fan. My family were of blue-nose stock and I attended games at Ibrox as a youngster watching the muscular Christianity of John Greig and the heading ability of Derek Johnstone. These were good times and I recall attending with my cousin the Cup Final of 1973 with over 120,000 inside Hampden.

My interest in Scottish football waned as a student, especially during three years in Oxford, though I recall roaming the streets of New York in the summer of 1983 while studying in Yale. There my eye caught sight of a *Scotsman* newspaper several days old with a front page celebrating the victory of Aberdeen in the Cup Winners' Cup. This was long before the days of the internet and smart phones, and news travelled slowly. I felt proud to be a Scot in Manhattan that day, though their achievement now seems from another era.

As a parish minister in the west of Scotland, I re-entered the raucous world of Scottish football. On one occasion, I visited a disaffected church member who was unhappy with the ecumenical practice of celebrating the seasons of the Christian year. He viewed this as a betrayal of Protestantism. In the course of our discussion, he delivered his knockout punch. "I suppose you're one of those ministers who think Rangers should sign a Catholic." He was right, but by the time this actually happened I had become a Hearts supporter.

Celtic visited Tynecastle for the opening day of the season in 1989 and I encountered a supporters' bus decanting a group of Hoops fans all wearing the same T-shirt. It sported a photo of Maurice Johnston clad in his Rangers top, sitting in the confessional. The caption read, "Bless me, Father, for I have signed." Football fans do irony better than anyone else.

I'm often asked why I converted to Hearts – always the bridesmaid, as the saying goes. It seemed simple enough. By 1986, I was teaching at Edinburgh University and my wife worked every Saturday as manager of a store in Princes Street. We lived in west Edinburgh. Looking for some entertainment, I regularly attended games at Tynecastle. Supporting the local team was something to do. Or did I feel sorry for them? They had lost the league and cup in that infamous week in May of the same year, but they still seemed good enough to win something. Or maybe it was genetic or atavistic.

My mother's father had been a Hearts' fan much of his life and celebrated their last success in the Scottish Cup in 1956. When I still *in utero*, Willie Bauld was scoring against Celtic at Hampden. Another factor was a friend who was a lifelong Hearts' fan – our wives attended school together in Lanark – and we decided to buy season tickets in the (old) main stand. When our children came along we brought them up in the same faith – a surprisingly easy task – and now they follow the team with even greater enthusiasm. In fact, they regard us as the two grumpiest fans in the stadium. Instead of a new singing section, they say that a moaning section should be opened in the ground where we can be immediately relocated.

One my predecessors at New College, Edinburgh, J. S. Stewart, was chaplain and a director at Hearts. He was regarded as the greatest Scottish preacher of his generation, though it was said that Hearts was the only subject on which you could engage him in small talk. In later years, he suffered from coronary disease and was advised to stay away from games to avoid unnecessary strain and excitement. This seemed the cruellest of prescriptions. I'm sure that he would have felt the better of a visit to Tynecastle. And in any case he lived and continued to preach into his 80s.

Football has proved a good male-bonding exercise in our household. I've attended games home and away with my two sons for about 25 years. We recall the defeats and victories in almost equal measure. Favourite mealtime discussions have revolved around questions such as, "Dad, who's the worst ever Hearts' signing?" or "What's the worst ever game/ground you've been to?" Given the vast number of plausible answers, these are tough but fascinating questions.

My wife has little interest in football but has acquired or suffered a comprehensive knowledge of the game from hours of conversation at the dinner table. Now a pharmacist, she can cheerfully converse with delivery drivers to their amazement on the latest injury list or transfer targets.

We're mighty fortunate still to be in business at Tynecastle following the debacle of the Romanov years. He took the club to the brink of destruction with reckless decisions that beggared belief. To console me, a friend once remarked that I should be glad it was only Hearts he now controlled, and no longer the firing codes to a nuclear sub in the Russian navy. But the sanity, decency and fiscal prudence that Ann Budge, the 'Queen of Hearts', has brought to the club have taken us into a new and brighter era. We have even acquired running water at half-time in the toilets at the back of the Gorgie Stand. Long may she reign over us.

Scottish football is an acquired taste. Of course, we know it's not the Champions League and I can soon produce a litany of complaints to anyone who's willing to listen to me. Why is there no game scheduled after New Year when we're all on holiday? Why are plastic pitches tolerated? When will Hampden be flattened? Apparently, one of my former doctoral students advises his successors that if ever they want to distract me from an indifferent piece of work, they just need to get me started on Scottish football.

Sometimes I meet people who tell me that they've occasionally attended a game and been so dismayed by the poor quality that they never return. But they miss the point. It's not about quality but about competition, camaraderie, the unexpected and the small victories that keep us going. And I've derived just as much enjoyment from watching and coaching primary schoolchildren as seeing Hearts lift the Scottish Cup, which proves the same point.

The banter that bonds supporters from across clubs is also part of the attraction. I took my kids to Firhill on one occasion many years ago. We were seated in the old stand. One of them spotted a dead pigeon in the netting above our heads and he asked me what it was doing there. When I mentioned this to a Thistle fan, he nodded his head sagely while remarking that it would be for the half-time pies.

The subject of religion and sport is one that is intensely studied nowadays. I have read books and once lectured on the subject, but in doing so I discovered that I prefer to keep these activities separate in my life. I suppose that I should write about the theology of football but somehow this would make it part of the day job. Sport is a distraction, even an escape. Success or failure are intensely experienced at football matches, but these emotions dissipate very quickly. Two days later the highlights of a game have already started to lose their appeal as the next match is anticipated.

This is the beauty of the exercise – it's great fun, endlessly absorbing, and a rich topic of conversation in the workplace, but somehow it doesn't really matter all that much. There are of course elements of quasi-religious adherence in football clubs – the bonds of affection, the rituals, the adherence to place and tradition, stories and songs about past heroics, the chanting and the cheering. I'm often impressed by how well and for so long many supporters can sing. For Hearts' fans, the volunteering of the great 1916 team remains a powerful story – having enlisted in Macrae's battalion, several died at the Somme, along with supporters of both Edinburgh clubs. I've sometimes thought that the church could learn from all this or some of it, though I recall a cynical colleague once challenging me with the Marxist claim that football is a form of false consciousness. Evidently, he'd never supported a team.

Sport is also infected with all manner of irrational superstitions – ways of preparing for the game, lucky mascots, and crossing oneself before entering the field of play. We don't bet in the church but perhaps a sweepstake on the next moderator of the General Assembly of the Church of Scotland would raise the public profile of the office. But the crossover with religion is a bit uncomfortable at times. I like to recount the story of Yogi Berra, the baseball catcher. When a hitter took up position in front of him and crossed himself, he said, "Why don't you just let God enjoy the game?"

Perhaps the most uplifting aspect of being a football fan is that each week brings something new. The old is soon left behind as disappointment quickly subsides, and by Monday you can start looking forward to the next game. In his book *Fever Pitch*, Nick Hornby remarks that no fan ever imagines dying in the middle of a season. You expect to stick around to see what happens and how it ends. But of course it never ends. That is part of the appeal – the most important game is always in front of you. There is something to anticipate, no matter how wretched the past. Hope persists in spite of expectation and bitter experience. Our love of football may just be a happy proxy for something better and more important.

David Fergusson is Professor of Divinity at the University of Edinburgh

Chapter 14

Diamonds Are Forever

Sandy Sneddon

I've heard many other supporters say it and I've said a few times my-self that you need to have faith to keep on supporting a particular team, especially one that struggles perennially to challenge for a league title, to go on a cup run, or even to play attractive football. Aye, you need to have faith to keep going to games when it's so cold you need two cups of Bovril to get you through 90 minutes. Aye, you need to have faith to watch this shower, couldn't lace the boots of the team back in the [insert decade of choice].

It was my dad who introduced me to football. Kicking a ball about the back green, later graduating to the park across the road. Taking me to games at Broomfield, sometimes treating me to a seat in the stand, introducing me to former players- turned- journalists who sat at the rudimentary press bench. Blethering to the guy on the turnstiles as he lifted me over in that time honoured tradition. Letting me know how important it was to keep supporting Airdrie and not Rangers like so many of my friends. I don't think I ever really knew why it was impor-tant, it just was. It just is.

And there were rewards for such loyalty. Like when my dad took to me to Broomfield to see Airdrie beat Nottingham Forest on penalties in a Texaco Cup 1st round game in September 1970, the first time a game had been decided by spot kicks in Scotland. Airdrie supporters of a certain vintage still talk about the night Roddy MacKenzie saved three penalties to send the Diamonds through to the next round.

Or the following April when he took me to Hampden for the first time. I was in awe of this massive stadium, I'd never seen anything like it. It was a Scottish Cup semi-final against Celtic, still a great team with a few Lisbon Lions lining up against my heroes. Airdrie were 3–1 down but got it back to 3–3 thanks to our deadly strike duo, Drew Jarvie and Drew Busby. Celtic won the replay but it was a memorable occasion.

Another great memory from that time was when Airdrieonians gave Sir Alex Ferguson the biggest defeat of his entire professional football career. It was two days before my 11th birthday as season 1970–71 drew to a close. Airdrie needed to score six against Falkirk and the final league game to beat Rangers for a place in the following season's Drybrough Cup. My dad wasn't long out of hospital after an operation on his back. As we left the house to go the game, my mum told me to make sure my dad was OK and if his back was hurting, we had just had to come home. Jarvie and Busby were again among the scorers along with a couple of legends in that team, winger Billy Wilson and that great leader of men, Derek Whiteford. The goals were flying in. I think Airdrie were 4–0 up when I dutifully turned and asked my dad id he was OK, just as my mum had told me to do. Gripping the terrace barrier with white knuckles and through teeth gritted with pain he replied, "Aye, I'm fine son!" No way was he leaving and we saw Airdrie run out 7–1 victors!

That was the last game I went to with my dad. Just over three months later he died. I think, like me, he would be bewildered at the indulgences and ostentations of parts of the modern game. The ever increasing transfer fees and salaries, admission prices that put the game at the elite level out of reach for many people, the subscriptions to TV coverage of more games than you can shake a stick at, the endless analysis in the media. A few years ago I thought about celebrating a big birthday with a trip to the San Siro or Nou Camp but the cost seemed extortionate. I didn't want to contribute to the excesses of the football at that level. I know people have been fretting about football being killed by its own extravagances since Alf Common was transferred from Sunderland to Middlesbrough for £1,000 in 1905 but you have to wonder about the sustainability of some competitions and the future of some clubs involved in such high finance football. I remember that Jesus spoke more about money than just about anything else in the Gospels. Sometimes it seems as if football is more about money than the game on the park.

I regularly go to games with my boys. They grew up knowing that Airdrie was our team – its important, it just is – and they have been ballboys and mascots, proud to brag to their schoolmates whose support for Arsenal or Manchester United meant they never went to games, never got a free pie for being a ballboy. My grandson comes to home games regularly and I even lifted him over the turnstile at Ochilview last season, grin on my face as I too partook of that time-honoured tradition.

There might be some similarities between the observance of faith and following an unfashionable, often unsuccessful football team.

There's the weekly ritual, the songs and chants, meeting friends who share your commitment. The passing on of it all to the next generation. But there are differences, huge differences. And I have long disagreed with Bill Shankly's line about football being more important than life or death. Yes, football is important to many people, it is easily the most popular sport in the world, many make their living from it, many more try and fail. Crowds great and small turn up week after week to watch games, pubs and clubs are crowded to see games on TV. I know my mood can be affected by the result come 4.50pm on a Saturday afternoon. But is a game. One I have enjoyed since childhood, one that has given me many joys, helped build friendships, and been a staple of probably too many conversations over the years. But it is a game.

I know I was star struck by Drew Jarvie, mesmerised by Madonna, in awe of Guardiola's Barcelona. I wished I had been at Wembley in 1977 or Mendoza, Argentina in 1978. I'll be at the Excelsior and Ochilview and hope to see my team soon at bigger, grander grounds, but none of these, none of this collecting experiences is what life is really about. The way to abundant life is not found on the way to a game on Saturday. I think football will always be part of my life, but I know it's only a game, a Beautiful Game at that.

Sandy Sneddon is a Church of Scotland Elder and has worked in Pakistan and Scotland for the Kirk's World Mission Council

Chapter 15

Scousers and Scots

Rachel McCann

I was born on Merseyside in 1971. By the time I first watched a match at Anfield, my Dad had convinced me that Scottish footballers, and indeed managers, were a superior breed! Bill Shankly laid the magnificent foundations for the Liverpool teams I saw, and those teams included some great Scottish players – Dalglish, Souness, Hansen, Wark, Gillespie, and one of my favourite players, Steve Nicol.

While across the park at Goodison, Gray and Sharp were in their prime. My dad idolised Shankly and would regularly quote him. He also idolised Souness and one of the highlights of his life as a supporter was when we went to watch the open top bus tour in 1984 when Liverpool had won a treble. My Dad shouted, "Well played Graeme", only for Souness to respond with a big grin and thumbs up.

Standing on the Kop was undoubtedly a spiritual experience – the ecstasy of a great goal (Dalglish curling one in), the emotion and unity of singing 'You'll Never Walk Alone', the sense of community and the joy of humour, not to mention the occasional prayer for divine intervention (especially if were playing Manchester United)! Anfield is a powerful place, as Shankly said of the fans, "I think it's more than fanaticism to them, it's a religion to the thousands who come here, come to worship, it's sort of shrine, it isn't a football ground." (1) And that's how it felt. His words certainly rang palpably and poignantly true when the Kop became a place of mourning and consolation after Hillsborough.

The Friendly Club

I moved to Glasgow in 1997, and while I carried on supporting 'The Reds', I sought a Scottish team to support. I had always wanted to visit Celtic Park and went to a brilliant match there with a great atmosphere. But it came as a shock to me to discover that Old Firm matches were not like the Liverpool derbies and the hatred and sectarianism scared me.

After talking to my then flatmate, I decided to support Partick Thistle. After all, they had given us Alan Hansen and Shankly himself had played for them during the war years while he was in the RAF. They were our nearest team, and my flatmate told me, "My Dad wanted me to be safe and to have fun at football, so he brought me up to support 'the Jags', because they are a friendly team." I lived in Maryhill for five years and although I didn't get to many matches it was always great to share in the local buzz when games were on at Firhill and I still follow their results and the work of their charitable trust.

Shankly believed that football was a force for good, and often spoke of his ideals and principles. "The socialism I believe in is everybody working for the same goal and everybody having a share in the rewards. That's how I see football, that's how I see life." These values can be seen in religion in its best expressions, and although it was very much Shankly's working class upbringing that influenced him, David Peace, the author of *Red or Dead* (a semi-fictional portrait about Shankly) said, "His form of socialism, probably going to back to Robert Burns, a biography of whom was his favourite book, grew out of his understanding of Christianity." Shankly had certainly reflected that "Burns was an early socialist – the first was Jesus Christ of course. He didn't think that God made people to be unequal, he thought everyone should share in the work and the rewards."

Although a lot has changed since Shankly's day, particularly the influence of capitalism in the sport, football can and is still a way of bringing people together, (rather than dividing them) and it can be a vehicle to challenge prejudice and to build community. Groups like Kick it Out, Nil By Mouth, Show Racism the Red Card and the many LGBTI+ supporters' groups have enabled changes and challenges to be made. I have recently been invited to attend the board of the Scottish Football Supporters Association (SFSA), and that is another important group seeking to influence football and empower supporters.

Walking Football is also a positive footballing influence, particularly in building friendships and helping to combat social isolation. It has taken off across the UK and here in Biggar we have joined over 70 other clubs in Scotland in starting a group. Women and men play together, there is great camaraderie and all of is have improved our fitness and skills. Rose Reilly – the only Scot to win a World Cup – is one of its patrons and it was opened by Minister for Sport and my MSP Aileen Campbell (herself a big football fan).

This summer myself and some of my Walking Football friends went on a wee pilgrimage, to Glenbuck in Ayrshire, to see the shrine dedicated to Bill Shankly. It was special celebrate the man and to see the place that shaped him and his philosophy so deeply.

Rachel McCann *is a former Youth Worker for the Iona Community*

Chapter 16

He's 'Oor Galoot': Following the Accies

David Adams

My dad introduced me to the agonies and ecstasies of watching professional football 'way back in 1947. It was just after the war, I was 10 and we were staying at my grannie's in Croftfoot waiting to get a house of our own. Just down the road was Cathkin Park a short bus ride away. My dad was an avid Rangers fan but the 'Gers were at Hibs that Saturday and Third Lanark –v– Aberdeen seemed a good day out. It was a pivotal moment in my life and a mistake on the part of my dad. He took me to see a team with a strange name, a team in red jerseys, a team that won 1–0 against Aberdeen. The die was cast. We were to 'share' many awkward moments when Thirds came up against Rangers in the future.

One game stands out for me, a mid-week Third Lanark –v- Celtic league match at Cathkin Park. It wasn't a great game and the Celtic fans around my brother and I amused themselves by hurling abuse at one of their own number (I cannot remember the unfortunate player's name) throughout the game. Suddenly my brother and I were forced into joining in, as this player, probably out of frustration at the constant bombardment from his own fans, lunged into one of ours and brought him down in a crunching tackle. We thrust our way to the front of the enclosure and gave him the benefit of our disparagement. There was a tap on my shoulder and I turned round to see a dapper little man sporting a smart overcoat, green and white scarf neatly tucked into his collar and a white bunnet on his head.

"'Scuse me boys," he said, "by all means support your own team but do not chastise our players. My big friend is getting a wee bit upset." He pointed to a giant of a man who was waving a finger at both of us with some menace and right away I realised one did not wish to upset this particular fan. "But you lot have been getting torn into him since the kick-off," I protested, "according to you he's an eedgit, a balloon, a galoot." He smiled as if in the presence of an idiot child, "Aye," he acknowledged, "but he's oor galoot."

There was a spell while following Thirds that expectations did rise to almost the levels shown by fans of the 'Old Firm' and that was in the late fifties/early sixties when Cathkin Park was the scene of many glorious victories with no small help from the famous inside trio of Hilley, Harley and Gray. They dismissed Hibs from the Scottish Cup (Gordon Smith and all), stood shoulder to shoulder with Rangers and Celtic, scoring 100 league goals in the process while still managing to only come third in the league. There was a wonderful attitude to going behind, "We just go up the park and score again." I said we scored a hundred goals; we also let in eighty. Brilliant stuff!

For a time, we had two Hilleys in the team as Davie was joined on the wing by his brother Ian. Sadly, not all fans liked Ian. One fan in particular I remember turning to me in disgust as Ian scored for the second time in a match and muttered, "That's a' that chancer's good for, scoring goals." As the teams lined up for the ensuing kick-off, he roared at Hilley the Elder, "You're still a dumplin'." Actually I believe scoring goals is quite a good trait to have.

There is a sense of belonging following a football team just as in any cause (worthwhile or not). Meeting up with mates each week is a major part of the attraction. I've often thought it strange in football that the team constantly changes, players don't stay fit for ever and good players move to bigger clubs yet I and those who see themselves as Accies fans attach ourselves to this team, which is ever changing, the club strip being the only constant, though now-a-days in the corporate climate in which we live, even that changes by small and sometimes horrible tweaks in a bid to sell replica strips every two years. As yet, Hamilton have not taken to the field wearing pink shirts. Now, I would need to think about that.

In 1973 I returned to Lanarkshire after working up north for just over 2 years. We settled in Lanark. I decided at this point to give up the refereeing and take the boy (my 11 year old son, David) to a match. Hitherto he had watched Highland League footie from the touchline, while I ran the line getting dog's abuse from the fans, usually both sets, which made me feel I must have been getting something right (or horribly wrong). Our first game was a Scottish Cup replay between Hamilton and Montrose. There was close to 11,000 fans in the crowd, a record attendance for the Old Douglas Park. Montrose won 1 - 0 with a twice taken penalty, but the seed had been sown.

At the start of the following season Accies had a pre-season open day. I attended along with my son and nephew and they got their pictures in the local paper with one of the Accies star players. The seed was now germinated; there was no going back. We had embarked on a sporting life that would go from amazing highs to abject lows with a fair degree of sheer mediocrity thrown in. One game stands out, and it's not the famous 1–0 win over Graeme Souness' all star Rangers in 1987. Again, it was against Montrose, in a league cup home and away tie. Montrose had won the first leg at Montrose 3–1. By half time in the return match they were ahead again leaving Accies trailing by three goals. An amazing second half saw Accies come back to win the match 7–6 on aggregate with three goals coming in the last two minutes.

As I leapt to my feet to cheer what proved to be the winning goal I became aware that my son was standing on the top rail of the front of the grandstand, scarf above his head and yelling his lungs out. I had this image in my head of telling his mother about this wonderful match we had witnessed and concluding with "Oh, by the way, the boy's in casualty, he fell out of the stand."

Nowadays, as a Hamilton fan, I follow the team more in hope than in belief that they will perform well. A good day out is not to get hammered by the opposition and, just occasionally, my devotion is amply rewarded. While I have never sought Divine Intervention to rescue a match, no matter how much I felt we were being sorely tried, I draw the line as far as Christian Charity is concerned in that sending the opposition fans home in a happy state is not a priority. It's more Old Testament "Get intae them!" when it comes to football although the referee in me demands that I see that it's not just the opposition players who are fouling, diving or wasting time.

Past results will mean nothing, every new game will be different even if the team out on the pitch is the same as last week, the performance will depend on each individual playing to his best. As an illustration of this I end with statistics of the Scottish Cup, Season 1986/87: Round 3 – Beat Rangers at Ibrox (1–0); Round 4 – lost to Motherwell at home (1–2). Faith? I could have bet on it.

***David Adams** is an Elder of the Church of Scotland*

Chapter 17

The Song of the Clyde

Graham Blount

I'm not sure what it says about me that after nearly sixty years I still have two of the gifts that marked my seventh birthday – a Bible and a Clyde scarf. But I do know which caused more excitement at the time, not least because my support was rewarded less than a fortnight later when Clyde won the Scottish Cup. My father had been taking me to Hampden to watch his beloved Queen's Park, but I had converted to the Bully Wee the season before when I discovered that this team who were breaking scoring records (in Division 2, but I was too young to get this nuance) played just down the road from us.

I didn't get to that 1958 cup final, but my dad took me to the first league game of the next season when the cup was paraded round Shawfield, and he held me up to touch it. That was me hooked, despite that early success of my support not having been repeated – so far; it isn't glory but hope that sustains us. The real impact of my support for Clyde may be seen in the drop from that cup win (their third in twenty years) to their more recent flirtations with dropping out of the league altogether.

Once I was old enough to get myself to Shawfield, I had a teenage season ticket, and there were good times there in the sixties, with us finishing third in what was then the first division in 1967 just behind the Old Firm. That should have meant qualification for Europe, but the Inter Cities Fairs Cup had a "one city one club" rule; despite our claim to be a Rutherglen team, not Glasgow, we were excluded – we thought Rangers were concerned we might draw crowds away from Ibrox to see us take on Barcelona and the like ... oh the cherished grudges!

In those heady days of Scottish prowess in Europe I had an exciting wee part-time job as "photographers' runner" at big games, sitting with them behind the goal and taking exposed films out to a waiting taxi. On only one occasion did Clyde figure in these – a cup semi-final replay against the Lisbon Lions of Celtic. I vividly remember watching as Bobby Lennox broke through on Clyde's goalie, Tommy McCulloch, who advanced only for Lennox delicately to chip past him. As the ball rolled gently towards the goal where I sat, I briefly thought "I could save that" ... but the moment passed, and I lived to tell the tale!

Years of study at St Andrew's reduced my Saturdays to following Clyde's ups and downs anxiously on the radio. I do remember one New Year carefully explaining to the Japanese student who was staying with us in Glasgow for the holiday (and therefore obliged to attend a ne'erday derby against Celtic) that we supported Clyde but did not go with realistic expectations of victory. A 2–0 half-time lead for us seemed to give a lie to our pessimism, but we ended up holding out for a brave draw.

My time in Bridge of Allan coincided with Clyde's "gypsy army" years with no home of our own. The complicated train journey to Hamilton was often beyond the time I had available, and I flirted with the heresy of Stirling County rugby, though Clyde was still deep in my heart. In Falkirk I had to contend with strong local identification with another "wee" team. When they hit the heights of a Cup Final against Kilmarnock, the Kirk Session hired a bus and I happily went along. As we approached Glasgow, police were stopping supporters' buses to check for alcohol; while one officer quizzed our organist/organiser, another came on board, took one look at us and our placard proclaiming who we were, and decided not to bother checking the racks!

By then, Clyde had moved into their new home at Broadwood, which I had proudly watched being built – all seated and a plastic pitch, both of which took a bit of getting used to. At an early home game, those of us unused to sitting to watch our team had to be reminded by tannoy that we could still cheer them on!

My next post was at the Scottish Parliament. When I was interviewed for that job by some Kirk high-heidyins, one asked – to my consternation – if I expected my application to be taken seriously. "Er ... yes" I stuttered, before he added, "in that case why, under hobbies, do you tell us you support Clyde Football Club?" My quick response comparing the role of Parliamentary Officer to that of a creative midfield player may or may not have been what got me the job.

Almost every talk I gave about my work at the Parliament ended with the bold assertion that being a Clyde supporter was my qualification for the job. Those who support big teams can go along and shout their abuse, to little effect as everyone is shouting and no one is listening – which might seem quite like the Westminster model of politics. But – as the great Willie Hunter once wrote in The Herald, comparing a Queen's Park home game to a Hampden international – with small teams, it is not just that the players (or even referee) might hear what you shout, but they may even do what you say! The moral of the tale, especially for a small Parliament, is don't write the letter that simply gets the frustration out of your system, but write one that might make a difference.

It was amazing how often this "coming out" as a Bully Wee fan brought a response from people whose father or uncle supported Clyde; at a Presbyterial Council of the Guild (no less) in Ardrossan, it brought a lady who told me proudly that she used to wash their strips.

As a father of two girls, I did my best to bring them up in the faith as I paced the floor singing the Song of the Clyde as their lullaby, and they were introduced to Shawfield at an early age. On a sunny spring afternoon, an elderly fan told me what a great place the terracing at Shawfield was to bring the weans – "plenty space for them to run about!" No terracing now, but three granddaughters all had Clyde babygros and were "baptised" into Broadwood before they were a year old (and therefore too young to say no). When the presence of one produced a first minute goal for Clyde, it sparked a suggestion she might become a mascot ... capped by a nearby proposal that she be made manager. At eight, and now a keen player at school, she recently came home proudly with a 'Man (sic!) of the Match' award, so may be well on track.

Sadly, our fourth granddaughter has missed out on this initiation. For all that Clyde has been in my DNA through thick and thin, the signing of an ex-international whom a court found to have committed rape, and who denied any wrongdoing in this, while the chairman proclaimed what a great influence he would be on younger players, crossed an offside line for me. My "letter to make a difference" resulted in a meeting with a board member and the club chaplain, but not even the requested club statement on violence against women; so I am currently in self-imposed exile from Broadwood.

Yet there is a Clyde-shaped gap in my life, and I still check the score, and feel the pain. Supporting a team is not a rational decision to be revised when things are not going well. Despite the let-down, hope remains: the Bully Wee will rise again, on and off the field.

Was it that early touch of cup glory that embedded this in me, or simply where I grew up, or a fondness for lost causes? One of our wee group of fans, during a season when things were pretty dire on the pitch, reflected that it was the meeting up with friends that brought him from Edinburgh to games. This is a club from which three directors attended the funeral of my great friend and fellow Clyde supporter, George Wilson, and printed the tribute in the programme. This is my team, the Bully Wee, and the song that I sing is the song of the Clyde.

Graham Blount *has been a parish minister and was the first Scottish Churches Parliamentary Officer*

Chapter 18

The Road to Dundee

Doug Small

Though we never had the Chevys or the Baptist Church
We had a choice of colours for a broken crutch

So sang Michael Marra in "Gaels Blue", his tribute to Scottish Blue Eyed Soul Boys. Being a Lochee boy of Roman Catholic pedigree, Michael had no idea of the reality. We DID have the Baptist Church in Scotland. But whereas Michael pictured Aretha, Brother Ray and Whitney, my brothers and I anticipated Sundays in Broughty Ferry Baptist Church, not with the longing to hear the soul-stirring extemporisations of Sam Cooke, but the mandatory wearing of the hated kilt. These popinjays at contemporary weddings dressed in Queen Victoria's music hall idea of Scottish manhood deserve the uttermost derision. "Kiltie Jeanie, Kiltie Jeanie" has never rung in their seven year old ears as they ran the gauntlet of their sensibly dressed peers.

The Baptists in Scotland have some fine principles: *The liberty of individual conscience in the light of the scriptures; the priesthood of all believers*. One could go on. Admirable stuff. But as kids, it seemed just to be a list of ways to separate you from your chums.

My wife, Sheila, still can't believe I didn't see a Disney film as a child. That didn't bother us - but to miss *The Guns of Navarone*. The Sabbath – so many kilted ways *not* to be playing football in Orchar Park. And, of course, there was attending The Football. It wasn't self-evidently worldly in the deepest dye of The Pictures. But pragmatically it wasn't going to happen. My dad was an energetic pianist and organist, a conscientious public servant; an admirable visitor of the sick. An Evangelical who, for a year, visited a young man dying of AIDS, when few others did. But he was never going to take us to the football.

My class at primary school had 45 people in it. Those were the days. One infers that 22.5 were boys. All supported Dundee FC. They had won the league. They had made the semi-finals of the European Cup. (it was once a good pub quiz question – "Which are the only two British cities to have provided two different semi-final teams in the European Cup"? Dundee and Glasgow. Sadly in the big bucks era, various English cities have gatecrashed the party). In some theoretical sense, then, I supported Dundee FC.

But in my early teens, came the advent of a young man called Dougie Inglis. By 'advent' I don't mean much more than that he came to live next door. Soon, we were kicking the ball about in the back lane to the rhythm of "Døssing passes to Seemann; Doug Smith (a centre half, of all positions, who's never been booked), scores a penalty".

I feared I'd never see these mystical Scandinavians and Scots bestride the hallowed turf. Until, at the age of about fourteen, Dougie Inglis' dad was allowed to take me to Tannadice. Admittedly it was 'just' a reserve game on a weeknight. Had I been offered the Hanging Gardens, the Colossus of the Helios, the great man-made mountains of the lofty pyramids, and the gigantic tomb of Mausolus, I'd rather have seen Wattie Smith (he wasn't Walter then) and Hamish McAlpine that night. Much is made of the first match and the irreversible attachment it bestows. That was me done for. Hamish and Wattie swung open the gates.

A curious aspect of a strait-jacketed upbringing is that once a little trickle breaks the dam, the whole edifice comes crashing down as if Barnes Wallis himself is at work. In a few weeks I had seen the Graduate, drunk a half pint of shandy in Monifieth Golf Club and was selling programmes at Tannadice. I had the worst stance – inside the ground. Fans buy programmes on the way to the match - inside they are after their peh. I didn't care a jot. I got in for free, was paid a tiny commission (I'd probably have done it for nothing) and (probably best of all) we collected our programmes in the Manager's office. Actually it was (Club Secretary) Mrs Lindsay's office, but it adjoined the Manager's and the door was always open – Jerry Kerr's pipe smoke poured forth. It was from that vantage point that I saw Jim McLean at his desk on day one. Heady days.

Dundee were marginally the better team back then, but there was no alternative to betting a shilling with Ian Gunn twice a year and probably coming out down. Even worse was indulging in the same non-Baptist practice with Bill Walsh – a Rangers fan. I don't recall winning much in that wager.

Dundee United fans get a bit of stick from their neighbours for being glory hunters. It depends on your age. My early years were not the glory years. Dundee had Charlie Cooke, Alan Gilzean, John Duncan, Iain

Phillip, Jim Steele. We had a certain amount of journeymen. However we also had Jim Henry. He had long hair. He won a Scottish League cap. A concept we have lost. He bestrode United's midfield in a pleasing manner.

Faith must be tested. Our particular forty days in the wilderness were six visits to Hampden. Six visits in the Scottish Cup final before a win. Two wins out of ten finals. A similar tale of woe in the League Cup. Diddy teams like St Mirren, Motherwell and St Johnstone just need to rock up for the first time and nick the trophy off us. Not for nothing was United's first and best fanzine called *The Final Hurdle*.

In a book of this nature, it is tempting to go looking for some sort of deeper truth in our test of faith. But for all the perceived bad luck or injustice in the national cups, we sneaked into the Nou Camp and stole a victory and, in truth, were well rewarded for the Hampden tribulations with great European nights. FC Monaco, Munchengladback – I would start boring the reader if I listed them all.

The Monaco reference can't slip by without again quoting Michael Marra. A 'Dee by persuasion, he still found time and inspiration to compose a paean to Hamish McAlpine – eccentric custodian of the sticks for the 'Dees' historical rival. Being Michael, he embeds a reference to Grace Kelly's visit to Tannadice. "There's Grace Kelly by Taylor Brothers Coal" - a somewhat down at heel advertising board.

What, then, of faith and fitba'?

Let's get a text in: "Three things will last forever - faith, hope, and love - and the greatest of these is love." 1 Corinthians 13:13.

My *hope* for United varies. Currently three seasons have been spent in the second tier with playoffs loaded against the team from the lower league. Similarly *faith* in managers comes and goes. Some seem like lovely blokes, but no-one ever called Jim McLean "a lovely bloke"!

But I have *Love*. It's completely arbitrary that it is for Dundee United and not Dundee. (I actually love Dundee FC a wee bit anyway). It is a love that, in common lineage, binds one to one's brothers, their kids, one's friends, their kids and often complete strangers. I recall a young man was being ejected from Tannadice by the constabulary. From over my shoulder came the broad Dundee observation: "eh kent him when 'e was at the skail – eh'd nae brehns then either". I wanted immediately to go for a pint with the speaker.

Love bears all things, believes all things, hopes all things, endures all things.

Endurance – that probably covers most of the above ramblings...

Doug Small, *a son of Dundee, is a semi-retired medical physicist. He lives in Langbank with his wife Sheila and a collection of Just William books*

Chapter 19

New Converts at the Coupe du Monde Féminine

Callum MacDonald

Inclusive and supportive, yet assertive and unapologetic; the #OurGirlsOurGame. hashtag adopted by the Scottish Football Association for the Women's World Cup in the summer of 2019 was well-pitched and used widely throughout the tournament. It's also directly at odds with the shameful history of that organisation's treatment of the women's game. Perhaps the nadir in this ignominious record was in 1971, when UEFA's 32 members voted on a motion to incorporate women's football within their associations. Only one country voted against. Wha's like us?

Rose Reilly (whose story is told elsewhere in this volume) didn't wait for anyone's permission or blessing to play the game she loved. Shunned by her homeland, talent and single-mindedness took her to Italy and she won the World Cup. As midfielder Leanne Crichton tweeted in the aftermath of the lassies' inaugural appearance at the competition 35 years later, "We don't play this game for acceptance, we play this game because it's ours."

When the team took to the field for their final group match versus Argentina, in front of a crowd of 28,000 at the iconic Parc des Princes, it was tempting to view the moment as the culmination of that long struggle to claim rightful ownership. It's not that prejudice and barriers don't persist, just that they are increasingly irrelevant, to be ignored or ridiculed. After a disappointing start to the tournament, Scotland had much to prove, but only in the context of qualifying from the group, against the standards they had set themselves, not to any bigots who would question or mock their right to be footballers.

"No Scotland, no party" has become a recurring refrain following the men's team in recent campaigns, as fans make light of our repeated failure to qualify. You could hear it in the streets of west Paris on match-day, only this time the cry marked our triumphant return to the fiesta. A piper led a procession along the boulevard towards the stadium, flanked by a familiar yet noticeably different Tartan Army. More women and families but still lots of retro shirts, kilts and regalia. Many of the same songs could be heard comin' down the road. Doe, a deer, a female deer.

Those present bore witness to a watershed moment in Scotland's cultural history, but for many the occasion also had a deeply personal resonance. As we approached the stadium, I struck up a conversation with a middle-aged, kilted man with "Ross 13" on the back of his jersey. He revealed he was the father of Jane, the top scorer in the squad, and I echoed his disappointment that she wasn't starting the match. When I mentioned I lived in the flat above her in first year of uni, he joked that he didn't want to hear stories of any Murano Street antics. I don't think he had nothing to worry about - I remember Jane being a dedicated, teetotal athlete, even at 18, while combining football with her studies. Her story is indicative of the commitment and sacrifices the players have made, not all of whom have always enjoyed the luxury of being a full-time professional.

It wasn't only for the families of the players that this moment was significant. Scotland qualifying brought great delight and pride for my mum, a committed feminist and lifelong football lover, so it was special to attend two games with her and my Dad. It neatly paralleled another family holiday in France in 1998, the last time Scotland's men qualified, and one of my formative footballing experiences. While I wasn't able to join my Dad for the opening game against Brazil, I tagged along for a distinctly less glamorous affair in Nantes. Aged 8 and suffering from a bout of flu, I threw up at a French policeman's feet before Yugoslavia's drab 1–0 win over the USA.

The match in Paris 21 years later would leave me feeling sick in a different way. Yet the early signs were promising. There had been positive noises coming from the Scotland camp in the build up to the match. Recalling Faddy's legendary strike on the same ground 12 years before offered a good omen. After a tight opening, Scotland got the breakthrough thanks to Kim Little, announcing her arrival at the tournament after subdued performances against England and Japan. By the time Jenny Beattie headed in the second early in the second half, Scotland were playing with zest and belief. Little was now dictating the play while Argentina struggled to cope with Caroline Weir's guile and vision. The imperious Erin Cuthbert, another who had shown only flashes of her talent in the previous two games, suddenly looked unshackled, bursting past defenders at ease. When she netted the third and the girls celebrated joyously in a huddle of resplendent pink, the tension dissipated. The night promised success - redemption, even. It was a strange feeling.

The prospect of Scotland progressing at the tournament felt seismic not just in its own right, but as a corrective to a wider malaise at international level. The women play for their own careers and their own achievements, so endless comparisons to the guys will likely mean little to them, but it's clear the nation carried hope of a much-needed tonic for the repeated failures of the men's team. After three decades of habitually qualifying but underachieving at showpiece events, followed by a generation in the wilderness, was a Scotland side about to make it to the knockout stages of a major competition for the first time ever? At 3–0 up with 15 minutes to go, even the possibility of going out on goal difference seemed unlikely. Lingering ghosts were set to be banished. The comical hubris of Ally's Army now over 40 years past and consigned to national folklore. We'd really shaken them up, even if we knew we wouldn't win the World Cup.

Appropriate, then, that it was at the hands of "the Argentines" that Scotland would endure their monumental collapse. Just as we glimpsed a brighter, more confident face, the same old ugly features were exposed. When Argentina pulled one back my first thought was how it would affect our goal difference. We looked a little tired and vulnerable, yet Shelley Kerr made no changes to shape or personnel. By the time substitutions were made, we were in crisis mode, hanging on at 3–2. The final few minutes rivaled any Scottish sporting calamity of yore. It was replete with a 2019 upgrade through the farcical VAR, as if the FIFA apparatchik had doled out this dystopian punishment to restore a threatened natural order. At first the tackle in the box was waved away, before a predictable and lengthy delay as the referee eventually decided to consult the video. Another excruciating pause followed before the inevitable awarding of the penalty. But Lee Alexander saves it! Relief. No, something's not quite right. The crowd are confused. The players are agitated. Another VAR consultation. Retake. Goal. 3–3. At least there's still 4 minutes of injury time, right? No - full-time. Scotland are out.

Cue the introspection and self-flagellation. And there's the Trainspotting memes about how it's shite being Scottish. Why does a tendency to bottle it - at least in team sports - seem etched in our national character, as if winning would spark an existential crisis? Did we have a right to feel unlucky? Yes. But did we largely have ourselves to blame? Absolutely. It would be patronising the players to pretend otherwise.

That said, it's important to consider the bigger picture. If Shelley Kerr and the players are due some criticism for their performance, they also deserve much credit for qualifying in the first place. For 70 minutes against Argentina, and in spells against England and Japan, they showed they could thrive at this level. Lessons will be learned by this relatively young squad to take into the Euros.

It won't provide much solace now, but they're also inspiring a bigger victory. Prior to this year my friend's wee sisters, aged 8 and 11, had been boycotting football because it was always "men playing men". But they were at the World Cup as new converts, along with thousands of other girls and women. They were joined by legions of French school kids at Scotland's match in Rennes, with their faces painted and leading songs and chants throughout the match. Just a shame the one heard loudest was "Allez Japon!"

Callum Macdonald supports Raith Rovers and wrote match reports at the 2010 Homeless World Cup in Rio de Janeiro. He blogs at: spouting-cave.blogspot.com

Chapter 20

Playing With the Same Baw

Mike Mair

If you asked me the cause of my addiction to football – evident in my readiness to watch a game anywhere from the local school pitches to the most obscure website for Bulgarian League matches – I would have to answer, "Because I played it." This statement requires qualification: I played it as a child, teenager and young adult only; I played it badly; I played it with a heavy leather ball on gravel pitches which meant that a fall on the ground could remove the skin from exposed bodily surfaces; and I had to rely on referees whose commitment to sturdy bodily contact permitted violent assaults on the most tender of organs. I don't think my testicles dared to descend into the war zone until I was nineteen and a half.

Above all however, I played it in the football boots of the 1950's. These were masterpieces of heavy leather with huge reinforced toe-caps, designed to control opposing players rather than the ball. It was like playing the violin gloves on. No matter how much I admired Stanley Matthews, Gordon Smith or Willie Bauld, as long as I was wearing these boots, I was doomed to imitate Willie Woodburn, suspended sine die by the SFA in 1954 for "indiscipline". Don't whistle at me, I told the referee, whistle at the boots.

(On one occasion Woodburn came off the pitch and said to his manager, "Boss, I think I've got a broken leg." "Dearie me," said the manager, "And whose is it?")

But that makes me sound tougher than I was. Because I went to a rugby- playing school, my first experience of team football, apart from the street, was with the Life Boys, the junior branch of the Boys Brigade, from which I graduated, age 12, to the Brigade. At that time the BB football league in Glasgow operated on the principle that the total age of a team should not exceed 158 years, which meant that if you wanted to include a 17 year old you had also to include a 12 year old. Nothing wrong with that you may say, but it meant that my 12 year old self had to face huge and sometimes skilful young adults bearing down on me with extreme prejudice.

I owed my immediate promotion into the team not to my skill but to my perfect qualifications for the unpopular left-back position:
(a) I could kick with my left foot
(b) I had no attributes that would make me useful in any other position.

It's reasonable to describe my performance in my first two games as execrable, and what's more I knew it. Spotting my difficulties and my shame, the coach asked me what my problem was. "They're bigger than me," I told him, "And better." He listened, went silent and then spoke, "Never mind son," he said, "They're playin' wi' the same baw!"

This hit me with the force of a revelation. The same baw! Forget their size and skill, and focus on the ball. Forget their height and strength, just look at that ball and aim for it. I became a relentless tackler, and won it often enough to realise that when I got it I'd no idea what to do with it. Still, all those kids who could dribble and pass were playing with the same baw. I could learn how to do the same. And slowly, I did.

Perhaps that's the reason why, although I'm built big, my favourite footballers are small, from Jimmy Johnstone to Luka Modric, because their focus on the ball has more than compensated for their size. It may also explain why I refused to support either of the Glasgow biggies, and gave my heart to the late lamented Third Lanark.

Of course, the coach's words were not only a revelation about football, but also about faith. My Christianity is based on love of Jesus and the challenge of becoming like him. Meaning to be like him in his love of God, his championing of the poor, the sinner, the outcast, while offering affectionate honesty to the rich, the righteous and the establishment; his astonishing openness to whomsoever encountered him; his readiness to pour out his life, generously, joyfully, completely.

But, "to be like him" – isn't that a destination too far for a grubby, selfish, greedy, lying git like me? How can I have the impertinence to demean the character of the Son of God, by saying I want to be like him? It's a bit like me at the age of nine announcing I wanted to be like Ferenc Puskas because I'd seen him play at Hampden.

But the coach's wisdom applies here also. "Never mind son," he would say, "Jesus was playing wi' the same baw." And that's true, because in spite of the repeated mess the Christian Church has made of his nature, Jesus was a human being. Like me. Like you. Like Lionel Messi. He was playing with the same baw, namely, his human self, and on the same pitch, namely, this world. If he could do it, I can do it, my neighbour can do it, even Donald Trump can do it. And if, however hard I try, I don't get there, I don't need to worry about displeasing God, since Jesus taught that God is delighted with his children, regardless.

As Third Lanark supporters always knew, it isn't winning that counts, it's the faith that you might. As they used to ask, "Why are Third Lanark players planting potatoes round the edge of the pitch?"

"So that they have something to lift at the end of the season!"

Mike Mair is an itinerant minister who has a website http//xtremejesus.co

Chapter 21

Shelley's Tartan Army on Manouevres

Liz Work

In the Summer of 2019, Liz and her daughter Anna and their menfolk Alastair and Andrew found themselves willing conscripts to Shelley's Tartan Army at the Women's World Cup in France.

We went to the send-off against Jamaica at Hampden, unfurling our huge new saltire announcing us as the "Sma folk o Ceres 1314" in honour of our village's supporting role in the inaugural home win over England at Bannockburn. Alastair, who had harboured an ambition since 1974 to attend a World Cup and spent many a soul-wrenching trip to Hampden over the years, was determined not to miss this for anything.

In true Tartan Army style, we went to the World Cup by a serpentine route: flight to Paris, train to Aix, hire car to Nice for the game. Liz and Anna bought Scotland tops at the airport and were delighted to discover they were actually shaped to fit. Andrew, whose knowledge of Scottish Football is already encyclopaedic, encouraged us to download the BBC documentary on Shelley and her squad for the journey. It was emotionally stirring preparation.

Arriving in Nice on the day of the game, we caused some mild alarm as, all kilted up for the occasion, we took sustenance in a restaurant full of Nice bourgeoisie having Sunday lunch. However, we soon dissipated their concerns with good banter and international relations. We ended up giving the staff our spare tickets for forthcoming games we wouldn't be able to attend. The fan zone adjacent to the provocatively named Promenade des Anglais was noisy and good-natured, a large posse of women from Buckie leading the singing. The England fans were largely drowned out by this but took it well.

We took one of a long line of buses to the stadium, squeezed in with families and unsegregated from "the other lot". We had brought small some small Scottish souvenirs and gave them out to children on the bus. At the Stade de Nice, we bumped into one my friends from primary school, whose daughter is in the squad, we had a chat with one of the Scottish photographers behind the goal, we draped our saltire over the barriers and we thoroughly enjoyed the match. It had everything: the auld enemy, a daft refereeing decision or two, falling behind and then roaring back in the second half. It also, of course, had a Scotland goal that we celebrated as though we had won the World Cup.

I (once known at school as "heid the ba' Hunter") reflected that the experience had been inspirational: "Having played a lot of football as a child back in the 70s and 80s I was not encouraged as the minority gender in the sport (I was one of only two regular girl players in the boys team and only tolerated to make up the numbers). I saw no future in continuing to play the game. Being present at the World Cup, I was very moved to see how far Scottish women's football has now come and hope it will go from strength to strength. I also see it as a symbol of women taking part more equally in Scottish society today."

Liz Work *is a former student footballer, primary teacher, and artist. She lives in Ceres*

Chapter 22

Shelley's Heroes

Ailsa Henderson

No mony Scots huv seen their team
score three great goals, an let them dream
that this time it wid be aa richt
that we'd be dancin through the nicht
that 'nineteen-six-nineteen' wid be
the day that we saw history
oor women's team wid turn a page
an get us through tae the next stage!

The thunderstorm that rummeled roon
an brocht the temperature doon
wi full ten meenits peltin rain
an hour afore the kick-off came,
was nae doot keepin Scotland cool
an able tae maintain their rule
ower Argentina – whit a 'coup' –
we only hud tae see it through
it widnae be much longer noo
Until the final whustle blew

Fur near three-quarters o the gemme
we cheered the goals by Kim an Jen
an shouted oot wi pride at Erin,
while Lee kept guard wi saves that were in-
spired an shuirly kept us in it...
C'mon, c'mon we've nearly din it!

Aa ower the field Leanne an Kirsty
an Lisa showed that they were thirsty
Wi Nicola, Caroline an Claire
an Captain Rachel they wid dare
they'd qualified, an they wur there,

they definitely wanted mair

An so did we, ah'll no deny,
a nicht like that ye cannae buy...

Tae think ah micht hae missed it tae
The Parc des Princes sae faur away
the only chance ah'd ever get
tae see us in a World Cup yet
the only problem – truth tae tell
ah didnae want tae go masel
whit ah needed was company
somebody tae share it wi.
so ah decided ah wis gonna
take ma sporty niece Fiona.

An sae it wis we played oor pairt
an sung oor herts oot et the stert
her Saltire fae her shooders hingin
giein it laldy wi her singin
ma tartan shawl, an me, nae less
were spotted by ma niece in Inverness!

An sae it wis – whaur wur we noo?
Aye – haudin oan tae see it through
when oot o naewhere there's a goal
an Argentina's oan a roll.
Aw naw, anither, whit's the time
Cmon, cmon yer daein fine
an then a penalty, VAR an aa
that stuff, an noo the nerves are raw

IT'S SAVED – we cheer an hug an laugh
but naw, VAR says the goalie's aff
her line, an Argentina's noo all set
An this time sure it hits the net.

An sae the team in dark blue strips
is tellin us we've had oor chips:
when aa gemme we'd been 'in the pink'

an suddenly in jist a blink
we're left dumbfoonert – whit went wrang
the road hame noo seems awfy lang.

But that's enough we'll leave it there
an Shelley's Heroes will repair
the damage done tae hope an pride
an re-emerge a better side.

This gemme we'll mind fur aa the best
o reasons, an forget the rest.
Professionals tae their finger tips
they wore wi pride their Scotland strips
they gave their all and we'll be back
ye cannae ask fur mair than that.

The end.
Naw it's no, it's jist the beginnin
o a great future fur Scotland's Women!

Ailsa Henderson *has worked for Oxfam and Christian Aid*

Epilogue

A Scottish African Tale

Iain Whyte

In 2016 the Homeless World Cup (HWC) was held in Glasgow's George Square. Fifty-two nations took part, including eight teams from Africa. African teams face extraordinary difficulties, funding, travel and the British immigration system that has often randomly refused them visas. The Zimbabwe team, managed by Petros Chatiza, travelled from Hatcliffe, one of the poorest communities near to Harare, where their project *Young Achievement Soccer for Development* has survived and benefitted young boys and girls for many years. Not all the players selected that year were allowed to enter Britain and take part in the Glasgow tournament.

One of the rules of the HWC, designed to promote the idea that all are winners, is that the host nation provides spare players to help teams that are understrength. This is when Joe from Glasgow found himself playing for Zimbabwe. Like many he came from a troubled background, and told me he had no idea where Zimbabwe was. But he threw himself into the task and this tall blond white guy soon became a brother to the Zimbabweans. Awkwardness vanished as Joe celebrated or shared disappointment with his new friends, getting alongside Blessings, who was profoundly deaf and only able to communicate by sign language. It was an eloquent plea from Joe that led to the referee putting a card back in his pocket when Blessings had put in a particularly hard tackle!

For Joe it was, as he said, the most 'magic' experience of his life. It gave new hope and dignity to him, and he was thrilled when his teenage son came to watch the Zimbabwe team. Joe's and Blessings' stories can be echoed in so many different ways. In Cape Town in 2006 the irrepressible Desmond Tutu with a huge chuckle, let the whole stadium know that he had heard "a rumour of a romance between a lad in the Scottish team and a young South African lassie."

David Duke, the founder of *Street Soccer Scotland,* gave me in 2009 a dozen jerseys for the project run by Martin Asamoah, manager of the Ghana HWC team. The Ghanaians proudly donned the Scottish strips them half way through a match that they were ahead and, you've guessed it, they lost! But, as Mel Young likes to say, "A Ball can Change the World".

About the Homeless World Cup

The 17th edition of the Homeless World Cup took place in Cardiff's iconic Bute Park, right at the heart of the Welsh capital, from 27 July – 3 August 2019.

More than 500 players representing over 50 countries travelled to Cardiff to attend the week-long festival of football, in what is one of the most inspiring Homeless World Cup tournaments yet.

This was the prospectus: "One of the goals of the Cardiff 2019 Homeless World Cup is to create a long-lasting legacy in Cardiff. In addition to aiming for maximum exposure of the event – thus changing people's perceptions and understanding of homelessness – the event also aims at providing employment opportunities in the run-up and after the tournament.

The Cardiff 2019 Homeless World Cup bid was led by Welsh actor and activist Michael Sheen. The event will be delivered by the Homeless World Cup Foundation in coordination with Cardiff City Council, Cardiff University, Cardiff City FC Foundation, FA Wales, Pobl Group, Office of Michael Sheen, Working Word, PYST and Street Football Wales."

More information about the past, present and future of the HWC can be found here: https://homelessworldcup.org

All net proceeds from this book will go to support African youth teams and associated development in association with the Homeless World Cup.

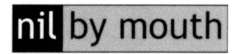

Challenging Sectarianism

About Nil By Mouth

Nil by Mouth is a registered Scottish Charity existing for the sole purpose of achieving a society free from sectarianism where cultural and religious diversity is respected and celebrate by everyone. We believe that Scotland can succeed in this goal if we unite together to tackle the problem as a nation.

Nil by Mouth is concerned with the destructive social impact that sectarianism has upon our lives and upon our society.

Nil by Mouth is based in Glasgow and works throughout Scotland.

Nil by Mouth is not a religious organisation.

Nil by Mouth is about challenging intolerance and prejudice

Nil by Mouth provides awareness raising workshops to schools, workplaces and other groups.

Nil by Mouth works in partnership with a variety of organisations and has been involved in many anti-sectarian projects over the years.

Nil by Mouth is a small organisation mainly made up of a group of volunteers who give freely of their time, skills and experience.

More information, news and campaigns here: https://nilbymouth. org/aboutus/

About SFSA

With nearly 72,000 individual and affiliate members across the country, the Scottish Football Supporters Association (SFSA) was established in 2015 to provide a platform for the ordinary Scottish football fan to have a say in the running of the game and its future in Scotland.

SFSA is a voluntary organisation funded by donations from fans and other interested parties who believe that it is essential that the interests of the key stakeholders are represented and that football clubs and the football authorities are held accountable to those stakeholders.

As well as producing and acting on a wide-ranging manifesto, *Transforming Scottish Football,* the Scottish Football Supporters Association has worked for inclusion, in support of refugees, and for football to be open to all – irrespective of ethnicity, class, gender, sexuality, dis/ability, religion or belief.

The national fans' organisation is free to join for supporter groups and for individuals who have a common aim of ensuring that Scottish football thrives for future generations to enjoy.

More information here: https://scottishfsa.org/about-sfsa/

Siglum

About Siglum

Siglum is a new imprint from Ekklesia Publishing which focuses on the illuminative and transformative possibilities of the arts, music and culture in both religious and secular contexts. Its logo is a dove, the universal sign of peace.

Further information: www.facebook.com/siglumpublishing/

Lightning Source UK Ltd.
Milton Keynes UK
UKHW010943191119
353775UK00002B/196/P

9 781916 173309